COME CLOSER

HOW TOURISM IS SHAPING THE FUTURE OF NATIONS

By
ANITA MENDIRATTA

ISBN-978-1-4507-5943-4

Visit website at www.anitamendiratta.com

For additional copies of *Come Closer*, please contact MyriadPublicationsInternational.com

First printing: February 2011

Cover design: Asher Hung www.asherhung.com

Cover image: Getty Images (Colin Anderson)

Print: Impressum South Africa

For Al, Aidan
and my Guardian Angels.

With love and thanks.

FOREWORD

DR TALEB RIFAI
Secretary-General, United Nations World Tourism Organisation (UNWTO)

Tourism has become a truly central global phenomenon. With over 900 million people crossing international borders every year, the sector is a clear manifestation of today's globalised world and proof that the 21st century is set to be the century of travel. What was once distant is now close; what was once different is now familiar; and what was once unknown is now understood.

Come Closer: How Tourism is Shaping the Future of Nations provides a sincere and comprehensive account of how, through tourism, people, businesses and nations are coming together in ways previously unimagined. Through travel we interact with different cultures and ethnicities, which in turn encourages co-operation and the creation of partnerships, bringing nations together. As *Come Closer* shows us, tourism is international diplomacy at its best.

Throughout the book, fictional stories are narrated, illustrating the main essence of each chapter and providing readers with a touching description of how tourism really can change lives. At the same time, this collection of personal accounts is complemented with theoretical guidance and information on developing a sustainable and responsible tourism sector; one that can deliver maximum benefits for not only those travelling, but also for the local communities visited and their natural and built environments.

This balance, between the hands-on and the theoretical, provides both the public and private tourism sectors with a complete understanding of the workings of tourism, both on the ground and at global level. *Come Closer* is thus an invaluable resource for tourism leaders, policy makers and stakeholders as they drive the global tourism economy forward.

Anita Mendiratta's ability to convey the importance of tourism in terms of its economic value comes second only to her capacity to reveal the very human side of tourism; the countless human interactions which represent the true essence of tourism. Having known Anita personally for many years, it gives me great pleasure to foreword a book that so clearly reflects her immense passion for the world of tourism.

UNWTO

World Tourism Organization

FOREWORD

GEOFFREY JW KENT
Founder and Executive Chairman, Abercrombie & Kent
Chairman, World Travel & Tourism Council

The World Travel & Tourism Council (WTTC) was established in 1990 when a group of business leaders of global tourism united to address head-on the fact that travel & tourism is the most important service industry in the world and the biggest provider of jobs, yet most people do not recognise how important it is. As a result, over 30 years ago the private sector made a commitment to work together to support the efforts needed to quantify the impact of tourism on national economies in order to raise awareness amongst policy leaders and decision-makers of its tremendous potential for creating wealth and generating employment. That commitment, which today reaches across the globe and the travel industry, remains strong.

In 2010 alone, more than 235 million people worldwide were employed in travel & tourism, representing 8.2% of all employment and 9.4% of world GDP. Employment is the most effective way to transfer wealth from rich nations to poorer ones. The travel industry provides good jobs, from the staff at airlines, hotels and restaurants, to guides and drivers, and the shopkeepers and artisans who cater to an affluent international clientele. Some of the most dramatic changes we are seeing in the international arena are from the emergence of Brazil, Russia, India and China as both host and source markets. These nations recognise the essential role that tourism can play in developing their economies.

Come Closer: How Tourism is Shaping the Future of Nations, authored by Anita Mendiratta, shares and effectively communicates the principles and practical knowledge that the WTTC has also learned about travel & tourism as a key economic driver. Travel can and does change lives and attitudes and, most importantly, build bridges between people. Sustainable tourism offers the best hope of protecting endangered places because it provides a compelling incentive to protect wildlife, habitat and culture. And most encouragingly, a new form of community development assistance is evolving from informal partnerships forged by the owners of forward-looking travel businesses who connect civic-minded travellers with local non-governmental organisations committed to making a difference in conservation, health, education and community development.

Importantly, *Come Closer* is a valuable tool for professionals within the travel & tourism industry, both business leaders and government officials, to understand the perspectives of both the public and private sectors. This cross-sector understanding is essential to ensure that government and business are able to effectively partner to promote and sustain industry growth. The WTTC is delighted to be a part of the worldwide release of this important book, and hopes that the global tourism community will utilise Anita Mendiratta's insights into the important role that tourism can play in developing economies.

WORLD TRAVEL & TOURISM COUNCIL

INTRODUCTION

This book is written to celebrate the times in which we live – times in which opportunity matters, possibility matters, mobility matters, understanding matters, legacy matters and compassion matters.

Times in which boundary lines matter less, differences matter less, distances do not matter at all.

These are times in which the world is hungry to reach out, spread out, to connect. To come closer.

Times where taking a flight means taking on the future. One traveller, one travel dream, at a time.

This book has been written as a labour of love.

It's not about you. It's not about me.

It's about the people whose lives will change for the better because of how the travel & tourism industry and the tourism economy are changing the world.

Because of how our working to grow travel and tourism is connecting the world.

Whether our focus is B2B, B2C or B2G, and working to support the UN's Millennium Development Goals, the G-20, our shared flag or individual businesses, our impact is critical.

Through our efforts we are doing our bit to build the travel & tourism sector, and therefore to build its future.

Now that is worth working for.

ANITA MENDIRATTA

PART 1
AERIAL VIEW

To be a leader in the travel & tourism sector today is to be an architect of future economies, societies and possibilities. This role is both an honour and duty. Ultimately it is an immense responsibility.

Reason being, with the borders of our world being erased through technology and ideology, travel & tourism has become a powerful enabler of identity and opportunity at both individual and collective levels. But there is a very real risk that throwing open a destination's doors to travel & tourism can be a greater cost than benefit. In selling the destination there is the risk of selling one's soul.

For this reason, this book has been written to examine carefully the various dimensions involved in establishing and advancing a tourism economy.

PART 1 of this book focuses on the *macro* perspective – the fundamental WHY behind tourism sector development.

Specifically, this section of the book calls out critical aspects of sector leadership at strategic and philosophical levels. Are all the answers to equitable tourism sector development held within the covers of this book? No, nor does it profess to. No single source can as this sector, and these times, are ever changing, requiring new ideas, new approaches and new solutions.

What this book does do, however, is pose the fundamental questions that tourism leaders should be asking themselves and their respective destinations, businesses and associations. These questions provide a compass to ensure we don't just do things right, but that we also focus on doing the right thing.

Because the fact remains that as tourism sector professionals, it is so easy to take for granted the remarkable rate of growth of the sector, and even allow growth to establish its own direction and momentum. Statistics become second nature. Focus shifts from insight and intrigue to facts and figures.

By first taking an aerial view, the essence of the opportunity of tourism sector development remains at the heart of all efforts of sector leaders.

Busyness is not always a good thing. We need to ensure that purpose fuels productivity.

And that the heartbeats of the people behind the inspired growth of the tourism sector continue to inspire our actions.

CHAPTER 1

IMPOSSIBLE POSSIBLE – WORLD SANS FRONTIÈRES

9:30 pm Saturday night. Time to get ready for the airport! Oh, he's almost here!

It is impossible for Joyce to contain her excitement. In just a few minutes Joyce's son's plane from New York City will land at Terminal 5, the new British Airways terminal at London's Heathrow Airport. It was at times like these that she found herself smiling, laughing actually, at herself. At thirty-five years of age, Max was still her little boy in her eyes.

She had prepared the guest room for him, and stocked the refrigerator with all of his favourites. He's coming home! And even though just for a few days, it would be wonderful. She wants to hear all his news. Every wonderful detail. This will be his first trip back since taking on his new job as head of JVS, joint ventures as he had to keep reminding her, at what sounded like a very impressive firm in the city. Though from what he tells her he is never at the office as most of his time is on the road, visiting current and prospective partners in Asia and the Middle East. To Joyce it sounded exhausting, all that travel, but clearly Max loved it. Kids these days!

No time to waste. She needed to get on the road, and get to the airport. He said he was happy to take the Heathrow Express into the city rather than have her bother with the drive, but she was insistent. Her boy was coming home – she will be there to meet him in arrivals. Mother's prerogative.

And truth be told, she was also very curious about this lovely new Terminal 5 she keeps hearing about.

Five terminals. Incredible. She remembers when Terminal 2 was added. And all the noise that created, even before it was built. The environmentalists versus the runways. Some things never change. And ultimately progress won out over protecting pastures. They say Heathrow is now one of the busiest airports in the world. She believes it! Traffic could be an issue tonight, especially considering it is a bank holiday weekend. But she will be there. Along with the rest of the excited arrival parties welcoming home friends and family landing from across the globe, all those exotic cities that will be covering the Arrivals Board in the terminal meet & greet areas.

She cannot help but smile, thinking of the first time she travelled to NYC. It was over 60 years ago... yet it is still so vivid. But back then flying was out of the question. It wasn't even an option. Her trip had been on a ship – a grand big ship that slowly carried her and her mother across the waters. It took eleven days. Today it is just an eight hour journey. In just eight hours she can cross the world!

Her parents firmly believed that more opportunity existed for their family by leaving their homeland, travelling to a place where opportunity was everywhere, for everyone. To travel, to expand one's world, was to better one's world. Whether in search of a new home or simply a holiday. The same principle applies even today.

Quite remarkable really. All in her lifetime. Travel, anywhere, any time. And now it is all at her fingertips. Her mother would never believe it. Imagine if she told her that just last month she herself had taken a trip to Europe for her grandson's graduation in Rome. Just three days away. And she booked it all just a week before, all by herself, all online.

It was that easy. Now, if only parking at Heathrow were as simple to make happen!

The map of the world today is an image in motion. Each moment, across the globe, landscapes are changing. A global process of reawakening and rediscovery is occurring, continuously.

Following decades of physical and psychological separation, monumental events such as the fall of the Berlin Wall and the end of Apartheid at the end of the 20th century, and the fall of the Bamboo Curtain at the beginning of the 21st century, have removed barriers that once kept people of the world apart. Changes in the world around us, changes that have created exposure where there once was closure, have changed the way we look at one another. And how we see ourselves.

In a single generation, our reference point for the world has changed. In the past decade alone, the world has become a universe of possibility. The emergence and empowerment of nations into the global economy has resulted in a dramatic redrawing of the map of the world. This redrawing has occurred not only in terms of physical spaces. More importantly the redrawing has occurred in terms of social and economic lines. Lines of connection, not division. Borders are being erased. Political lines matter less, connections are mattering more.

And with that, profound shifts of power have occurred. Where once the West was the centre of commerce, opportunity and possibility, today the lens of the future is shifting east. BRIC nations – a term originally coined in 2001 by Jim O'Neill symbolising the shift in global economic power away from the developed G7 economies toward the developing world, namely Brazil, Russia, India and China, collectively, this force of nations has redefined where future growth will occur in terms of wealth, spending power and investment attraction. For the period of 2000 to 2010, strikingly, the growth of stock markets in the BRIC nations amounted to greater than forty percent per annum, while stock markets in the EU and US actually contracted. Similarly, the share of BRIC nations in the number of listed companies worldwide jumped from just over 2% in 2000 to 22% at the end of 2010.[1] Even in recent periods of global financial crisis, BRIC nations were able to maintain focus and momentum, showcasing the strength of their foundations. In 2009, while the world was tightly held in the vice of recession, global equity-market capitalisation rose nearly 47.1% to reach US$ 47.9 trillion.[2] Of this, BRIC nations showed the strongest levels of growth, with market capitalisation more than doubling.

Not far behind in the quest for hyper-growth are the N-11, Goldman Sach's term for the next eleven emerging nations (Bangladesh, Egypt, Indonesia, Iran, Mexico, Nigeria, Pakistan, the Philippines, South Korea, Turkey and Vietnam). Where once global dominance was defined by political muscle, today it is about purchasing strength. Capitalism and consumerism have taken over where communism left off. Nations once restricted from participating in global conversation, in thought and/or action, have become lead voices as a result of liberalisation of policies and politics. And these voices have become stronger, younger, sweeter and more social.

To be a child today in an urban centre in China, or India, or South Africa, or even Russia, is to grow up in a world apart from that which existed just one generation before. Today, with a single keystroke, the world is literally at one's fingertips. More sophisticated, more accessible and more welcoming then ever before, the world is open for friendships, for business, for whoever wants more.

Because today, all around us, opportunity and possibility are omnipresent, simply waiting to be embraced. The days of difference have passed. Who we are, how we relate to one another, and the responsibility we have to the world around us, have become active thoughts. And active debates. The question 'why?' asked by the previous generations has been replaced by the bold statement of 'why not!' by today's youth. This is an empowered generation seeking to discover the world because it's there.

This new global community is wonderfully curious. Cultures, countries and characters previously unknown or not understood are being actively explored. To learn. Unique to our times, now, with a simple keystroke on a computer, the world has opened up – people's lives, loves, cares, concerns and convictions can be tapped into with speed and intimacy never known before. And with that comes true insight.

Understanding of other people and places is now but a mere click away. As are worlds once off limits due to expense or ideology. As long as one can log on, the global community is a place to belong. And for over a billion new global citizens, the world is a place to see...and to be seen.

But seeing the world through the web, as a Google traveller, is just the appetiser to seeing, touching and feeling the world close-up.

Which is why, in parallel to the opening of borders through technology has come opening of borders to travel.

Since the turn of the century, the global travel & tourism industry has experienced overwhelming growth. Without a doubt travel & tourism has become a powerful form of expression and empowerment, for both individuals and nations.

Travel has always carried with it a natural cachet. Not only does travel reflect financial capability, it also reflects mindset. With travel comes insight, wisdom, knowledge, know-how and bragging rights. Where people go, how they get there, why they go and what they bring back in terms of stories and souvenirs – it all says something about the traveller.

Now, at a time when significant populations of the world are finding themselves finally able to proudly stand up and, with passport and ticket in hand, travel the world, not only does travel demonstrate where one can go... it also shows that one has arrived!

Similarly, as global citizens act on their dreams and desires to explore parts of the world previously unchartered (and possibly uninviting), nations once closed off to tourism are enjoying the experience of welcoming travellers to their shores and doors. Whether they are arriving for leisure or business purposes, visitors to travel destinations have come to represent a wave of new interest, opportunity, investment, identity and growth for nations.

At an individual level, each and every day, from East to West as well as West to East, millions of people are excitedly boarding planes and trains, travelling to places once only dreamt of. The dream of travel in a world previously closed off, either economically or politically, has unlocked a new generation of discovery.

As a result, an awakening has also started to occur on the receiving end within the workings of national growth and development. Opportunity is arriving. Not only is it knocking on the door – at times it is buying up the door and the entire building. Because it can.

This wave of opportunity and activity is both exciting and daunting. Where will the wave lead? With what force will it mobilise change? How will it impact the lives and livelihoods of all those in its path? However it may be viewed, it is happening.

Importantly, it is getting nations working, and it is building futures.

For destinations opening their homes and hearts to people of the world wishing to make a connection with new places, joining the global tourism sector has mobilised a labour of love – a love of country, identity and possibility.

Without a doubt, tourism has become a global golden child. Ranked as one of the fastest growing economic sectors in the world by the UNWTO, tourism has become one of the most powerful forces of international understanding, accessibility and unity ever known.

The world is on the move. Each and every day, over 7 million people travel internationally, crossing borders and flight paths, journeying between countries and cultures. Over 70 million people travel each day within their own borders. Collectively, in 2010 alone, the UNWTO estimates approximately 935 million in international arrivals, a staggering movement of people from one point on the map to another. People of newly liberated nations have begun to explore places, cultures, ideologies and opportunities beyond their borders. Holidaymakers are seeking out discovery of more intriguing and story-inspiring roads less travelled. Global business centres are excitedly shifting from west to east. And advances in aviation are enabling people to be anywhere they wish with higher frequency and lower price.

For destinations themselves, tourism, unlike any other sector, unlocks the opportunity for a nation, region, or locale, whichever the case may be, to look good, feel good and create good.

Tourism acts as the gift wrapping of a destination, showcasing the destination's most stylish, compelling and inspiring aspects and putting forward a confident, caring invitation to travellers to come visit for work and/or play.

By marketing and promoting a nation's God-given natural beauty, its history, its lifestyle, its culture and the spirit and hospitality of its people, governments of even small, newly established countries are able to establish a name and place on the international tourism map right alongside the world's largest, longest established, leading tourism destinations.

However, unwrap the gift wrap and the real gift of tourism is revealed.

Tourism, once viewed as an industry based on play, pleasure and passionate patriotism, has finally established profile, respect and credibility around the globe as a powerful driver of the economic engine of nations.

The numbers speak for themselves. Currently generating over US$ 1 trillion per annum in direct earnings (indirect earnings being as high as three-fold those of direct earnings), tourism provides nations with a proven, solid source of revenue. No other industry can yield such high levels of income with so little initial capital investment requirement.

Of critical importance, the people of the nation have the opportunity to play a part in the growth and development of their home. From bead artists creating handcrafted souvenirs for today's tourists to Tourism Authority Board members creating a masterplan for the destination of tomorrow, people of all walks of life are able to participate in the tourism industry. Each and every individual has the ability to touch, and be touched, by tourism.

Globally, there is no faster growing sector of employment. At present the tourism industry employs 10% of the people of the world, unlocking hope and opportunities for the future of the people who call the destination 'home'.

But evolution is not only about the numbers – arrivals, revenues, length of stay, dispersion, repeat visitation and all of the other metrics which the industry uses to quantitatively measure performance.

Growth is also fuelled by the importance of travel & tourism at four core levels:

- **Economic:** The travel & tourism sector has become a phenomenal earner of revenues for destinations. In addition to the money, which travellers directly inject into the places to which they travel, the sector has proven its ability to be a powerful attractor of investment. These funds, be they FDI or other, are then able to be channelled towards the development of essential infrastructure needed by the destination for tourism sector development, as well as general infrastructure which the people who call the destination 'home' can benefit from. Mass transport systems, airports, ICT networks, safety and security services, sports and leisure facilities, hotels and attractions. All of these areas of destination engineering receive strong support from investments made to uplift and increase the competitiveness of the travel & tourism sector.
- **Political**: The travel & tourism sector has become a valuable driver of the strengthening of the focus, fabric and future advancement of nations. Governments across the globe have recognised the importance of the sector in the unification and development of both the economic and social dimensions of the nation. In defining the travel & tourism sector as a priority of the government of a destination, political leaders of the destination begin the process of shaping the identity and core objectives for growth.
- **Social**: Flowing directly from the above, the travel & tourism sector has proven to be invaluable in bringing together people of the destination around a shared national identity and invitation to the world, regardless of age, race, religion, profession, personality and political point of view. The low barriers of entry to the sector make it possible for all people of the destination to play a role in the tourism community

and economy. Be they artisans, architects, advertisers, travel agents or government advisors, everyone has a valuable part to play to ensure that the destination truly works to deliver a unique, compelling and competitive tourism experience which will sustainably attract visitors for business or leisure travel purposes. And importantly, as tourism experiences are delivered primarily through SMEs (small and medium enterprises), the sector makes it possible for parts of society in emerging nations which were previously unable to join the workforce to make a contribution through their skills and initiative. As a result, the sector empowers more and more citizens to play a meaningful, recognised role in national growth and upliftment.

- **Psychological**: Over the past decade, as the world has flattened and perspectives have broadened, travel has become a core psychological need for both individuals and companies alike. Travel is no longer about movement from logistical A to B. It is about social movement, economic movement, spiritual movement, and the movement of cultures closer to one another. As an example, since the Bamboo Curtain has fallen billions of new capitalists have entered the global community with great excitement. Travel has become a vehicle for showing oneself, and others, who I am. And when it comes to business, it has become essential in breaking down barriers and out of date perceptions about who we used to be. In addition to playing a part in one's individual identity, travel has become a form of personal therapy – the opportunity to escape, experience, exhale... whatever the need may be in these increasingly stressful times.

Tourism provides nations, large and small, with a platform for wealth creation and nation building.

The rewards of tourism, therefore, go far beyond revenue calculations and investment recovery ratios.

The real richness of tourism is in what is unseen. Tourism creates a magnetic bond of identity, pride, confidence and promise between people of a destination. And in so doing, tourism strengthens the social fabric of the destination. Harmony, appreciation, respect, co-operation, productivity and shared success all create a spirit and sense of identity for the destination which, for the travellers, strengthens their understanding of the destination. The traveller is able to go beyond what there is to see to discover what there is to be felt.

At a societal level, governments are reassured that their people are working together towards a more prosperous, promising future for themselves and their families, built on a solid past and sense of the present.

The shiny image that a destination projects in its advertising and marketing, and the experiences that a destination promises to travellers, magically and meaningfully gift wraps the economic operations of the destination, creating an excitement for the future.

And as with all gifts, the joy is not just for the traveller receiving all that the destination has to offer. The joy is also felt by the people of the destination who proudly share their special part of the world with its visitors, knowing they are playing an important role in the growth and development of their home through tourism.

CHAPTER 2

INTERNATIONAL DIPLOMACY AT ITS PUREST

It was only 5 pm but still there was a chill in the air. As soon as the sun went down it was as though a little heater was turned off – immediately it felt colder. Another Irish winter was definitely near.

But Sheila was not yet ready to leave her book and perfect Sunday afternoon spot in the window seat of her lounge. Not just yet. All she needed was a little blanket to keep her warm while she finished the last pages of the chapter.

Sheila instinctively reached out for the rust, red, green and gold pashmina that she bought in Pakistan. A real pashmina, down to its last fibre. She adored it. Her husband, John, had bought it for her at a little market in Islamabad when they were in Asia last year while she joined him on a business trip. Not a usual get-away spot. Quite the contrary. Which is what made it all the more special.

Holding it now in her hands, breathing in the scent of the wools, touching the soft threads of the yarn, feeling the sunshine of that day held in the golds and reds of the design, it all comes back to her. She remembers vividly seeing an elderly woman with a wrinkled face full of stories weaving it in the marketplace. It was not finished yet. For at least half an hour Sheila kept watching the woman as her old, tired hands danced around the threads, like an angel playing a harp. Sheila's husband watched his wife taking in the scene, and knowing how she valued such moments, such living postcards, he offered to buy Sheila a pashmina. Sheila was deeply touched.

But she wanted that one, the one that was made by the old woman with the musical hands...

And so they waited, returning the next day to the market, looking purposefully for the stall, bending down gingerly to meet once again the pashmina artist disguised as an elderly Pakistani villager. They did not barter – they paid her what they felt the pashmina was worth.

Visibly taken aback by the kindness of these strangers purchasing her pashmina, the artist slowly reached out and, with her own fragile hands toughened by years of weaving and weathering life's storms, took Sheila's hands and shut her eyes. Sheila could hear her whispering something in Arabic: "Rabbanaa baarik laka wa usratuka bil khair wal hayaa wal siihah".

It was a prayer. From the words he could make out, John whispered to Sheila that she was wishing them health, happiness and peace.

Receiving the spontaneous blessing from the woman, holding that moment in their hearts as she and the artist held hands, she and John knew they had done something far greater than purchase a souvenir. They had helped a family.

One trip, one market, one exchange, one story. A lifetime of impact.

The reality of the world today is diverse, dramatic, divergent and at times, deeply troubling. Our world has become increasingly connected through 24/7/365 technology that we willingly invite into our lives anytime, anywhere and anyhow. To be connected has become a reflection of our hunger for information and appreciation. Our sense of responsibility and productivity is increasingly measured by volume of messages, strength of networks and speed of sharing of opinion.

Global communications lines have played a critical role in erasing borders. Communities are created across the globe based on what one represents as a thought, regardless of what one represents culturally, nationally or demographically.

And yet, for all of our connectedness, still global issues and opinions have us not just moving further apart, but often pushing apart. A single, seemingly simple comment about one group of people from another can spread like e-wildfire, enflaming opinions and even actions. The more easily accessible and bloggable international commentary has become, so too has the risk of hyper-acceleration of judgement. Sadly, and often, opinion is without pause for fact-checking and verification, or careful consideration of consequences. For all we are learning about the world through our inter-connected lives, at the same time we are unlocking how much more we still have to learn.

This is particularly relevant when it comes to understanding people from other countries and cultures. Just why do certain nations and their people do certain things certain ways? Why do they hold certain beliefs? What makes them certain that their way of life is affording them the best possible opportunity for development as a society, economy and national or cultural identity? Why do these people think in certain ways about other nations, other ways of life? Why do they wish to be closer to us? Or stay far away? Certainly there are reasons?

To try to understand different nations through facts and figures would not only be an exhaustive, academic process, it would deprive us of one of the most critical elements to understanding other people – nations and cultures – of the world: a heartbeat.

For anyone wishing to understand the ways of other people and places, wishing to scratch below the surface of details and definitions to uncover real insight and wisdom, there is one 'school' which provides greater richness of learning, true understanding, than any website or wondering can offer.

It is a remarkable way of gaining understanding which penetrates not only our minds, but also our hearts and our lives.

Through tourism the world has developed a platform for people of exceptionally different locations and viewpoints to come together.

A platform for creating enduring awareness, respect, appreciation and even affection. A platform for releasing judgements in favour of embracing truths seen, heard, felt. And a platform for peace.

Today, in these rapidly-changing times, there is no other economic sector which actively and enticingly encourages an individual from one part of the world to willingly invest his or her time, funds and emotion into picking up and travelling to a completely different location on the globe to meet completely different people, become immersed in their completely different way, and return home with completely reshaped impressions.

It is only tourism that inspires such a quest for understanding and experience of differences.

In addition, one of the breathtaking aspects of tourism is the speed with which understanding and connection can be gained. Years of technical information about a culture cannot replace the split-second insight attained through cultural first impressions.

We have all experienced it, be it through travel to a neighbouring city or state, or to a nation a world away. Most often it is first felt through a smile. A smile accompanied in some parts of the world by a bowing of the head, in others a coming together of the hands in a gesture of prayer, in others a placing of one's hand on the heart. Words spoken may differ but the spirit is shared. "Namaste". "Salaam Alaikum". "Nĭhăo". "Howzit". "Howdy". "Cheers". "G'day". "Jambo". Whatever the case may be.

In a heartbeat, faster than definition can be Googled or Binged, understanding is there. The message is clear. "Come closer".

With that first greeting, be it from a flight attendant waiting at the doors of the aircraft to take you to your destination, or a taxi driver waiting on your arrival, or a hotel doorman waiting to welcome you, or a child on the sidewalk simply looking up at this new face in his neighbourhood, facts and figures become feelings. The mind widens to learn more, the heart opens to grow more.

With this growth comes connection. With this connection, a bond is formed, even if at the most simple level. With this bond, difference becomes dissolved.

And diplomacy is lived.

From that moment onwards, a place once defined as 'foreign' starts to become familiar. Frequency of hearing, seeing, sensing and being turns contrasts into comforting curiosities to be explored.

Wonderfully, and before we know it, initial assumptions are left back at the hotel. Days become spent soaking up not just the climate but also the living culture of the place – details which once were on paper or computer screens are now brought to life, in technicolour, in ways which truly make sense and matter.

When the time comes to leave, precious keepsakes taken back home are the stories of times spent with local people, in their space, in their own way. Clear recommendations for friends/family/colleagues are formed of what they need to do, see, experience, when they come on their trip to this wonderful new place with its wonderful people. Why will these people also visit? Because the recent returnees will insist – they will insist that headlines not be taken as defining of a people, that judgements are not made without experiencing for oneself, that opportunities to experience the beauty of differences and finding similarities not be missed.

As aptly stated by Bruce Bommarito, Senior Vice-President and Chief Operating Officer of the United States Travel Association, USTA:

> *"Tourism is the ultimate form of diplomacy."*

Intuitively, we know it. In addition to being a powerful driver of social and economic growth of nations – GDP, trade, FDI, employment, etc. – tourism has become a force for global good through its ability to act as a driver of diplomacy.

Through tourism, nations meet, cultures connect, people share, understanding is formed. Tourists – those curious to see what opportunities for understanding and growth are available across the world as business builders or holiday makers – become unofficial diplomats for their nation. Tourists, symbolising the people of the place they call 'home', become national representatives.

Mirroring this, the people of places visited become friends through simply being who they really are, naturally. In so doing, perceptions are shifted... for the better.

For this very reason, destinations opening their doors to tourists, for both business and leisure, must always looks at their citizens, and their visitors, as ambassadors of their flag. The way in which visitors experience the destination forms the basis of the way in which they will share their stories with the people in their world. These impressions are the seeds of connection. The more genuinely the connection is felt, the more endearing and enduring the connection will be.

To travel is to touch, and be touched.

And in these times of electronic connectivity, how reassuring it is to know that through all the wires and across the web, a simple smile from across the globe can remind us of how truly connected we all are.

CHAPTER 3

THE ROLE OF GOVERNMENT

Sixty seats. All lined up to create a giant oval with a giant conference room. Meticulously each seat had in front of it a microphone, a bottle of imported mineral water, a carefully selected glass and a clear sign of respect and deserved high regard: VIP – Reserved. These were where the Ministers of Tourism will sit. Layered behind them will be their respective entourages – Deputy Ministers, Special Advisors, Director Generals and Deputy Director-Generals, Aides, loyal followers. This global summit on Tourism Development was important. Because when these leaders, these minds, these centres of power come together, the global industry takes a step forward, together. And being a part of it was important.

Having followed the stream of global leaders into the room, Kim readied for what was ahead. Sitting positioned in his 'Advisors' place as directed by the nation-alphabetic seating chart, in anticipation of the deliberations to take place over the next two days as detailed by the official agenda, he could feel a faint smile in his heart despite the official, almost stern look on his face. Back home, back in Europe, the commitment to working for tourism through government can lose a sense of purpose, a sense of pulse. Policy, petty politics, prolonged debates take over. It is human nature. It is government nature. But moments like these had the ability to bring one back to the core.

And then the keynote speaker stood to take the podium. A new face. A new Minister of Tourism. A new leader rising from a nation rebuilding, refocusing on the future after a decade of war. Young, yet clearly confident. Open, yet clearly focused. Ready, and clearly excited. His expectant audience sat waiting, wondering how he planned to address the challenges of his bruised nation. If he actually could.

For the next twenty minutes he did not make a speech. He did not state mandate and policy and rhetoric. He did not try to charm this audience of powerful peers. All protocols were observed, absolutely, all respect was conveyed. But instead of making a speech he made a plea. A simple plea. "Believe in my country once more." As he spoke it was clear – his is a nation dependent on tourism to uplift its people, its history, its spirit and its future. The war may be over but the economic battle had just begun. Only through tourism would his nation gain the recognition, respect, appeal and active appreciation that it so desperately needed to come to life again. To be all it is meant to be – economically, socially, politically and spiritually.

As the volume in the Minister's voice rose, taking with it the energy of the room, back in his assigned seat Kim could feel it – that feeling of an inner flame being fed, feeling it lift, lift, lift, until it was pushing the corners of his mouth into an open smile, his eyes squinting with an inner sense of conviction.

This is why he does it! This is why he loved tourism! This is how he feels he can truly do his part to help change the world for the better.

At the heart of governments across the globe is the desire to unite people behind a shared sense of identity and purpose as a prelude to the creation of a stronger, safer, more secure and more rewarding future for generations to come.

For a nation to come together with a common desire for growth, prosperity and harmony, and as true believers in the promise and potential of their country, an immensely powerful vision is required. This vision must be able to touch people of all ages, beliefs and backgrounds. And it must offer a sustainable source of focus, inspiration and motivation for all.

When a government takes the strategic decision to embrace tourism as a key driver of social and economic growth, something very interesting starts to happen. With this decision a nation makes a pledge to open its doors to the world, hosting curious minds and hearts of people of all walks of life on its home soil. Citizens become ambassadors, culture becomes national character, places become pride-filled attractions, experiences become stories, and strangers become friends.

The travel experience, one that often has an enduring impact on the traveller far beyond the return journey home and sharing of stories around the dinner table, always has an enduring impact on the growth and development of the travel destination itself. It is impossible for a region or nation, for any destination, to open its doors to the world and remain 'untouched'.

However, the 'touch' of a traveller can be positive or negative.

With relatively low barriers to entry onto the global tourism stage compared to other high-return industries, the excitement around tourism has the ability to unite people of all parts of society, all sectors around the transformation of their 'home' into a highly compelling and competitive tourism destination.

As stated earlier, tourism brings with it rich, seasonal injections of exposure, excitement and foreign exchange. These exports increase greatly the attractiveness of the sector, inspiring destinations around the globe to invest in sector promotion. International travel & tourism trade fairs from Berlin to Beijing have become centres of rich concentrations of colour, fantasy and promise. And they have become forums of intense commercial activity and competition.

The business of tourism has become very serious, very lucrative, very fashionable and very aggressive.

However, for all of the rich rewards of tourism, there are also great risks. And these risks are real, immediate, penetrating and potentially irreversible: risks to the environmental sustainability, risks to greater economic stability, risks to local culture, risks to social value systems, to name a few. Simply put, in buying into the tourism phenomenon, a destination can face the risk of selling its soul.

Which is why it is fundamentally believed that

to enable the tourism sector to truly work for the destination, clear, visionary, focused leadership by government is vital.

Importantly, people from across the destination, people of all ages, skill levels, backgrounds and beliefs have, through tourism, an opportunity to actively and meaningfully participate in the sector in a way which empowers and inspires the people, economy and future of the destination.

This is not, however, by chance.

The energy generated by tourism is a result of a vision, an inspiring view of what the destination can become as a result of tourism.

Underlying this vision must, however, be a clear, comprehensive plan – a definitive HOW of destination growth and development.

At the heart of the tourism sector, as all good business thinkers know, must be the presence of a solid tourism strategy providing the framework for fulfilment of defined, measurable objectives. For as individual as tourism is, nations transforming themselves into compelling, competitive and clearly differentiated destinations must establish strategies, systems and processes to ensure that the sector can indeed deliver against specific tourism objectives.

But the development and growth of a successful tourism sector is not simply about a successful tourism strategy, no matter how brilliant the strategic thinking. The strategy is key. Without it the destination risks throwing its doors open to the world and, for lack of better words, selling its soul – losing its culture, character and care for one another for the purpose of making money through tourists. Cross messaging, cross purposes, crossed wires. Ultimately cancelling out opportunity.

Strategy is to a tourism sector what sheet music is to an orchestra. It is the direction, the focus and the framework.

But it is merely paper – ink on lines with huge promise and desire to create something beautiful – until brought to life through the hands, heart and eyes of the orchestra conductor. For the tourism sector that conductor is the government of the destination, the source of vision, inspiration and disciplining direction that turns passion into proud, purposeful, clearly positioned tourism marketing and experience excellence.

Why is the involvement of government really necessary when in many ways tourism is a relatively easy industry for anyone living in the destination to participate in? Advertising and marketing agencies know how to successfully promote and advertise. Travel agents know how to successfully sell holidays. Hoteliers know how to successfully run hotels. Restaurants know how to successfully serve fabulous local meals. And artisans know how to create curios and other keepsakes for tourists to buy and take home as gifts. Why is it necessary for government to play a part?

Simply this: tourism is <u>not</u> purely for tourism's sake.

To operate effectively for long-term benefit of the destination, government must mobilise the tourism sector as a critical driver of the greater:

- economic,
- social,
- cultural,
- industrial, and
- infrastructural

development of the destination for its people and their future.

As shared by Marc Collins, former Minister of Tourism of Tahiti:

> *"Nature and history have combined in a very remarkable way to create what many visitors in the last two and a half centuries describe as a true paradise on earth: Tahiti. However, this reputation alone did not guarantee that our tourism developed harmoniously and in lock step with the population's need for employment and the country's ambitions for development and growth.*
>
> *The government's role today is more than ever one of responsible stewardship and enlightened decision-making. The sheer beauty and fragility of our islands' ecosystems demand that the government truly devote the time and energy to find the wisdom needed to make the right decisions, then act decisively and consistently to attract investment, while protecting the environment.*
>
> *Tahiti's past was primarily written from the visitor's viewpoint. Tahiti's future will have to be written by Tahitians, led by a strong and wise government."*

Like the conductor of the orchestra, the government of the tourism destination has the greater:

- sense of vision,
- competitive market intelligence,
- executional insight,
- ability to align others, and
- access to resources.

These vital attributes turn what is on paper into passionate, purposeful, integrated performance that most consistently and creatively attracts target audiences who will most appreciate, and most enthusiastically visit, the destination.

Generally speaking, leadership of the tourism sector by government is required at two fundamental levels:

- **MACRO**: Establishment of overall tourism strategy and policies to ensure sustainable growth and development of the sector at social, economic and environmental levels, and alignment of sector efforts to the greater national/regional growth mandate.
- **MICRO**: Brand leadership of the destination, ensuring creative, co-ordinated, competitive and compliant marketing, promotion and innovation of the destination.

Working in harmony, these two dimensions of tourism leadership ensure that the vision of the destination is brought to life through its daily expressions, ie. destination brand promise, destination promotion, experience offerings, product and service delivery, policy implementation and infrastructure re-investment.

To fulfil the MACRO needs, governments establish Departments (Ministries) of Tourism to take high level ownership and responsibility for defining the long-term direction and impact of the tourism sector, including policy, participation and governance. It is these Departments and Ministries of Tourism which are best placed to ensure that the sector strategy for tourism is directly aligned to, and supportive of, the greater national economic growth, development mandate and strategy.

In addition, the tourism strategy needs to ensure that the stakeholder community is aware of, endorsing, and actively contributing to the fulfilment of the goals and priorities of the destination.

The importance of the stakeholder community, both public and private sector role-players, cannot be underestimated.

Stakeholders can be the strongest enablers of sector advancement when a shared vision is in place. On the flipside, they can be the most challenging barriers to tourism growth if visions and commitment to delivery are absent. It is the responsibility of government to take the lead in engaging, inspiring and enabling tourism stakeholders as true partners in destination growth.

Ultimately, government must act as a central leadership force for the tourism sector – its industry, community, partners and principals – providing a central source for destination:

- strategy,
- policy,
- investment, and
- stakeholder alignment.

Complementing the above, at a MICRO level the creation of National Tourism Organisations (NTOs), also referred to as Destination Marketing Organisations (DMOs) and National Tourism Authorities (NTAs), have become important levers for long-term, meaningful, optimised growth and development of the destination. Each destination, however, has its own unique needs and priorities when it comes to the growth and development of the tourism sector. Form follows function.

Through their destination marketing and promotional efforts, the NTO must ensure that the brand and marketing strategy for the destination are directly aligned to, and supportive of, the greater tourism sector mandate for economic growth and development, which in turn must drive that of the cross-sectoral national/regional mandate.

Each musician plays his or her own part, in accordance with the sheet music shared by all members of the orchestra who, together, are creating something truly spectacular.

For this reason, when preparing for performance, and as each note is played, government must continuously check that all essential elements are in place for delivery of a harmonious composition.

Questions that need to be asked, and re-asked, include:

- Is the vision is clearly defined?
- Are key stakeholders engaged and able to contribute to strategy formulation?
- Are strategic priorities understood in terms of tourism sector growth and greater destination economic and social development?
- Are the deliverables clearly defined and correctly assigned, with clear metrics?

- Do sufficient resources exist, namely people, funds and time, to enable delivery?
- Is progress being shared with role-players and the wider stakeholder community?

and

- Is the strategy being regularly reviewed to ensure alignment to destination vision and the greater competitive landscape?

In the end, as diverse as tourism destinations are in terms of:

- positioning,
- proposition,
- profile, and
- experience promise,

they share the need for inspired, visionary, comprehensive and carefully co-ordinated leadership.

Just as the conductor is responsible for carefully guiding his/her musicians towards the creation of musical magic as one united force, government must confidently lead the people of the destination's tourism community.

With a clear vision of the future of tourism for the destination, government must provide direction and inspiration needed by all people of the destination to live, and love, the destination they call 'home'... and proudly share with audiences around the world whom they know will truly love their art.

CHAPTER 4

TOURISM TERMINOLOGY

"But what do you mean, Sir?" she asked, looking at him with complete seriousness. Her question seemed to only frustrate him more.

"As I said, we must become a centre of biodiversity, demonstrating that through tourism essential marine and land life are in balance."

"But what exactly do you mean, Sir?", Vivienne repeated patiently.

He could feel his patience starting to reach its limit. But he knew he could not show it. She was only trying to help. And they say she is the best when it comes to speech writing.

The national budget speech was in less than a week, and he was not happy with the latest draft. He felt it would not reach people the way he wanted. The facts and figures were all there, but he could not feel anything. So he called her in. He needed her to find the words to inspire his people into action. Not only was it important to his portfolio, it was important to the island. And its whales.

Unable to answer her, locked actually in frustration, he began looking out of his office window, out across the beautifully tended tropical gardens now overflowing with pink and yellow hibiscus flowers from the recent rains, out past the line of palm trees which naturally lined the shore, to where he could see a ribbon of blue in the distance. The ocean. No matter where he travelled in the world, there was no sight that brought him more comfort.

Since he was a child he had been looking out across the water, waiting patiently, waiting for a sign. Even now he could feel his eyes instinctively squint just a tad, as though he were standing on the shore, waiting for it. Oh! There it was. A puff of spray. A whale!

What he did not know back then is how important those magnificent whales are to the island. Back then he simply admired their massive beauty. Now, as Tourism Minister, he also admires the massive impact that the whales have on the economy of the island. Especially at this time of year when they return to these shores to give birth to their young.

The annual whale migration and calving period brings with it a migration of tourists from across the country and world. Over the past decade, this influx of tourists has played a critical part in creating a thriving tourism industry – creating jobs, livelihoods and, importantly, pride. All this just because the world wants to see their whales – these beautiful creatures which have chosen his island as the first home of their young.

But to keep the island growing strong, sustainably, he needed to ensure that the tourism industry remained true to its roots, true to its whales.

"Sir, we need to move on, please. What do you mean?"

"I mean that if our island is to grow, we need to ensure that we invest in environmental sustainability for the sake of economic stability. We must ensure that conservation is a strategic pillar of our development plan".

"I hear you, Sir, but what do you mean? Why does it matter?"

With quickness of expression, almost regrettably, he blurted out: "Because Mother Nature has chosen our island as the nursery for her baby whales. And so we must protect it for her."

Startled by the speed and emotion of his words, cautiously he looked across the desk at her.

And to his surprise she was smiling.

"Then say that, Sir. Say exactly that."

The 21st century is becoming defined more by what we have been losing than what we have been gaining. As the world's rainforests, glaciers, icebergs, endangered animal and plant species, time, oil reserves, investment revenues and hope have proven less and less than we ever dreamt possible. The fear and fight for natural resources intensifies. Energy is being lost, tangibly and intangibly.

And yet there is one source of energy that each and every individual in the world has at his or her disposal, in abundance. This form of energy has the power to ignite simple ideas into sophisticated innovations, passing thoughts into powerful actions. From this source can come growth, development, legacy, unity, purpose.

This source of energy? Words.

Within the travel & tourism industry, an industry that has gained massive awareness, appreciation and participation across the globe over the past decade, our words have become a vital source of energy for the sector's success.

The words we use to lead the tourism sector in the destination – how we articulate our vision, our purpose, our goals, our unique identity, our challenges, our challengers and our future – are little bundles of energy.

This word-based energy that has the ability to:

- ignite a passion for the industry,
- inspire our actions,
- align our thinking, and
- create a strong, united, equitable, admired and competitive destination for the benefit of both the people coming to the destination as visitors and the people of the destination as proud residents.

This is of great importance in parts of the globe seeking to achieve upliftment and identity through travel & tourism. As has been proven time and again, the sector acts as a critical driver of the economy of nations, especially those defined as 'emerging' economies. In recent years the sector has moved away from initial consideration as a peripheral 'soft economy' on the outer fringe of economic impact and is increasingly seen as a 'hard economy' at the heart of GDP-based nation building.

Much of this is due to the fact that the sector has started to overtly describe itself, and be described by other sectors by words common to the dictionaries and discussions of economists: *trade, investment, receipts, revenues, % GDP, % Capex, yield, ROI, employment, equity.*

Still, new words and shared language do not necessarily mean shared understanding. Take the words *growth and development* as an example.

Every individual working within the travel & tourism industry seeks to achieve growth and development for their part of the tourism experience chain. Whether working within the public sector or as a private entity, in a budding SME or in an established corporation, focus and measurement of success are within the context of growth and development of the tourism sector.

Seems straight forward. Right? Wrong.

For those in government, *growth and development* refers to advancement of the sector through sustainable growth in visitor arrivals, GDP, job creation and equitable transformation. All of these contribute to meaningful destination competitiveness. Brand strength is also a critical part of *growth and development.*

For those in emerging small tourism businesses, the SMEs that form the fabric of the industry, *growth and development* refers to the creation of new opportunities for employment, for wealth creation, for ownership, for long awaited and hard fought empowerment through tourism.

For big business, *growth and development* refers to growth in margins, market opportunity, profitability and brand equity.

These are but a few segment-based comparisons.

Approaches to climate change and environmental sustainability also factor into the macro definition of *growth and development.* As do product development, the elimination of the highs and lows of seasonality, skills development and service excellence of our tourism experience delivery.

And of course there is the *growth and development* of sub-sectors within the travel & tourism industry – cultural tourism, cruise tourism, medical tourism, etc.

Three simple words, *growth and development*, suddenly unlock an array of different meaning. And, therefore, opportunity for understanding, and misunderstanding.

Misuse and misunderstanding of language is not unique to tourism. It also occurs in other sectors.

Within the tourism sector specifically, many words within our industry vocabulary have sadly lost their value of meaning due to:

- burden of political subtext,
- marketing overuse,
- association with specific leaders/times,
- boredom of usage, and
- default usage.

As a result, the sentiment and significance of what needs to be said is either defused or disappears alltogether. With it goes clarity, conviction and communication. The energy becomes stale, sterile and even sometimes cynical.

This is not a fate which must be accepted. Redefinition and reinvigoration of meaning is always possible. The renewable energy of words simply needs to be unlocked.

The opportunity exists for each and every individual in the travel & tourism sector, public sector and private sector alike, leaders, followers and observers, to bring meaning back into communication through careful usage of words:

- turning NOUNS into VERBS,
- finding NEW EXPRESSIONS of old themes, and
- EDITING out the sources of anything but inspiration.

As an example, the following wordplay demonstrates how official language can be adjusted to get both the substance and the spirit across.

T&T Terminology		***Alternative Expression***
Tourism Industry	→	*Tourism Economy*
Tourist/Traveller	→	*Guest*
Transformation	→	*Shared Opportunity*
Mandate	→	*Commitment*
Growth	→	*Advancement*
Barriers	→	*Challenges*
Strategy	→	*Critical Choices*
Goals	→	*Priorities*
Empowerment	→	*Enablement*
Tolerance	→	*Acceptance*
Responsibility	→	*Duty, Pride*
Advertising	→	*Communication*
Spend, Cost	→	*Investment*

Simple adjustments with potentially significant impact.

The tourism industry is the backbone of many nations dependent on the tourism economy for economic growth, social unity and global competitiveness.

What is said is the fuel for what is done.

Interpretation has a profound effect on a people's ability to create impact.
Therefore, when members of the tourism community speak to one another, sharing goals, aspirations and challenges, it is critical to ensure that the language used is bringing the industry closer together through shared understanding, vision and definitions.

CHAPTER 5

TOURISM INVESTMENT – INVESTING IN THE FUTURE

"Oh my, it is just breathtaking!" she heard her inner voice exclaim. Just as they told her it would be. Just as this particular part of the Alps was always known for.

Sharp, majestic, snowcapped mountain ranges reaching to the skies, skies filled with what looked like a scattering of cotton balls onto a beautiful blue canvas. And down below, between the carpet of lush, green grass and fringe of fir trees along the base of the mountain, a stream. A stream with water so clean and clear it looked to be fresh from the rains. Purity brought to life!

But what really made her smile was her timing. Spring had indeed sprung. And all around, as far as she could see, were daisies. Daisies, daisies, daisies! It looks as though God had simply spilled buckets of paint from the sky. Oranges and pinks and whites and purples. Thousands of daisies, all in a patchwork, a natural work of art. A sight so breathtaking that trying to capture it in a photograph would be a futile effort.

How can a place be so naturally blessed... and yet so cursed?

What was not visible to her naked eye, yet was hidden behind the overgrown brush, was the evidence. But she knew it was there. Like a wound hidden behind a layer of clothing. Still hurting, still healing. Still needing time.

She remembers reading about it in the newspaper back home. The world was watching, for a while at least. Until the next story broke.

It happened so quickly. With the end of winter's ice-cold temperatures and spring's overzealous arrival of above average temperatures came the floods. The cocktail of sunshine and snow created torrential downpours of water from the summit which, by the time they reached the village, caused devastating damage. It seemed at the time that nothing was spared. Hundreds of trees were struck to the ground, crushing all which lived beneath it. Mud seemed to swallow up all which dared step foot in its unconcerned, uncaring path towards the valley.

In its path, sadly, stood the valley's only real form of income, independence and identity – its tourism industry. Ski chalets were turned to splinters, trails to mud treks. The resort was a wreck. The village had all but vanished. And the homes of all the people who called the valley 'home', the people who had lived their lives there, were left in ruins.

But hope was rising just as the daisies were breaking through the ground in an effort to grow anew.

In the distance she could see the site of what her tour guide said was a resort development. They started building about a month ago, quickly moving in to turn five hectares of flood-crushed land into a lavish five-star ski haven. It should be up and running in time for next year's ski season. Excellent.

She shifted her glance to the area where the village used to be, all that now stood below the mountain range where mountains of rubble were piled. The clean-up was underway. Soon hotels and homes would replace the heaps of evidence of recent devastation.

The area looked rather like the arrival ground of a nomadic tribe – temporary buildings, trucks, generators, cranes and concrete mixers. New lines of tyre tracks marked what would soon be the major road bringing people, possibility and productivity back to the village and its new resort.

And standing proudly beside it all, a massive sign covered in logos and flags – partners investing in the rebuilding of this special corner of the world, this specially sought out ski spot of the Alps.

Taking in the scene she did not doubt for a moment that this village would not have seen such strong rebuilding effort if it had not been for the region's tourism industry. Building would have occurred, bringing the village back to life for the villagers who have built their lives and livelihoods on these slopes. But not so soon, with such determination and such planning. Clearly it did not only make social sense to rebuild – it made business sense.

Her thoughts were suddenly broken by the whistle of her tour guide calling her back to the bus. Time to go.

Looking through the window at the fields of flowers carpeting the mountain pass she could not help but smile.

If the daisies could talk, they would be singing.

The great recession of 2008/9 cost the world dearly, at many levels. As the first rumblings of trouble were felt in Q3 and Q4 of 2008, analysts the world over feverishly started to explore what exactly was going on.

How could the house of cards be falling so quickly and widely as a result of defaults on housing payments? Soon, with much shock, the symptoms pointed their arrows to the cause: credit – the passing out of too much credit, at individual, institutional and international levels.

As a result, 2009 took on a global identity as the year of the Credit Crisis. From the start of the troubles, numbers became the focus: how much money was being lost, how many jobs were being eliminated, how many businesses were closing, how long would this last? On the surface, the credit crisis was all about the numbers.

As 2010 unfolded and reflection on the losses took place, one thing became very apparent: our recent pains were caused by much more than excessive spreading of credit in the monetary sense. They were also caused by too much credit being given out in terms of emotional currency. In the end, institutions, individuals and even investments around the world are facing severe losses in credibility.

Looking back, as credit dried up at both monetary and emotional levels, investment into development came to a grinding halt. Cranes stopped spinning, cement stopped pouring, workers stopped building, architects stopped designing, bankers stopped loaning, visionaries stopped dreaming. No matter how grand the plans were, the risks were unavoidable.

The global travel & tourism sector had started to see significant investment flows into tourism and general infrastructure development. Governments enjoyed a period of strong investment attraction through FDI (foreign direct investment), JVs (joint ventures) and private investors. Similarly, private developers were able to secure liquidity through banks and private funders. The benefits of investing were deemed high, risk low. There was every reason to believe that the 4% to 8% annual growth rates of tourism markets seen in 2006 and 2007 would continue through 2008 and beyond.

With the credit crunch came the collapse of personal and business traveller flows, air capacity, yields and overall travel & tourism sector performance. Unsurprisingly supply of credit that had once come easily to developers of travel & tourism projects such as airports, attractions, resorts and the like, was frozen. Confidence and momentum of construction behind the sector, from resort developments to roadworks, hit a *cul de sac*. Across the globe programmes critical to the advancement and competitiveness of destinations had to down tools.

With the global financial community having declared the recession statistically over (if not yet emotionally), availability of credit and opportunity for investment are set to resume. With this comes the return of opportunity for the sector to resume its efforts to build a stronger, more solid destination proposition, and in so doing, provide critical strengthening of the wider economy of the destination.

The fact remains that resumption of development efforts is not simply a case of releasing the 'pause' button. So much has changed, from the business climate to the business environment, and the resulting business models are required to generate secure, sustainable results, especially within the travel & tourism sector.

From a developer perspective, it is clear that governments and private sector entities investing in the tourism sector must ensure that the fundamentals of their development plans are in place so as to be transparent of the opportunity for investors.

This principle is well understood in one of the world's leading regions of tourism investment and infrastructure development. As expressed by Diana Ee Tan, former President of Raffles Hotels and Resorts, current Board Member of Singapore Tourism Board, Member, Advisory Council, School of Hospitality, Republic Polytechnic, Singapore and the Academic Board of SHATEC Institutes:

> *"Singapore has established a global reputation as a world-class business hub and a competitive leisure and business travel destination. Central to our success has been creating a remarkable business infrastructure and valuable investment opportunities for visionary developers. Packaging such opportunities in ways which speak to investors, in their language, understanding their demands in terms of quantifiable returns, and engaging them as business partners have contributed immensely to the growth of Singapore as Asia's and one of the world's most trusted and inspiring investment destinations."*

This includes, on the tourism sector demand-creation side, clarity of:

- destination growth strategy, targeting carefully segmented source markets,
- destination offering,
- existence of a clear, competitive destination brand,
- investment in destination marketing and promotion,
- invitation to travellers – leisure and business,
- ease of accessibility: entry visas, air/sea/road access, year-round,
- uniqueness of experiences, attractions and local interactions,
- momentum of activity (ie. events) for ongoing traveller attraction, and
- effective travel trade co-operation and co-ordination.

And from a supply side, having in place:

- capacity and yield management of:
  – airlines
  – accommodation
  – attractions,
- skills development: hospitality and general service industry,
- safety and security,
- in-destination public transport services,
- supporting services: healthcare, banking, retail, and
- quality measurement and assurance.

As with all development initiatives, a sound business plan must provide the foundation for future building. Government and private sector leaders of travel & tourism sector development programmes must reassess viability of plans to ensure that what is envisaged and emotively promoted is in fact capable of providing sustainable, equitable growth and competitiveness for the destination.

At the same time, what must be taken very seriously by governments and private entities seeking investment from outside parties, be it foreign direct investment (FDI) or other forms of investment, are the fundamentals from an investor perspective.

The global investment community can be expected to look with sharper eyes at not only the travel & tourism sector investment offerings being made available by destinations committed to growth and development of the sector, but the investment and lifestyle environments in which they will reside.

As expressed by Juan Carlos Ventura Pimentel, Director of Marketing and Strategic Communications in the Ministry of Economy of the Federal Government of Mexico:

> *"Tourism activity fosters economic activity, including valuable trade and investment, throughout the world. The generation of revenue from visitors which goes back to the local community, directly improving living standards, also causes the emergence and growth of entrepreneurs and business developers. Thus, as infrastructure, services and communication channels are improved and promoted, they attract continued investment, facilitate the exchange of goods, and promote foreign trade. This contributes to the promotion of the destination as a place to settle companies and services of all kinds, creating more jobs and sectors of opportunity for economic development. At the end of the day, a business climate which offers prosperity, style and high quality of life automatically makes a destination a desirable climate for investment."*

As a result, governments, in particular, must ensure the following ten dimensions are taken into account when trying to secure the support and commercial commitment of the international investment community once more.

The travel & tourism investor check-list below provides a basic framework for promoting investment opportunity by governments.

It is also, in fact, a way for the destination to carefully and honestly examine what effort it is making to ensure investors are getting all of their needs fulfilled – a way of responding to an investor's natural question of *"What are you doing for me to make it worth my time/money/energy here?"*

The Travel & Tourism Investor Check-List:

- **Stability:** Strength, certainty and capability of the government leading the nation, providing reassurance of investment safety and longevity.
- **Security:** Assurance that investment funds are being utilised exactly as committed, that they are generating expected returns, and that investors are able to take earnings out of the country if and when desired.
- **Systems:** Presence of reliable, trustworthy systems essential to effective investment mobilisation, ie. banking, legal, fiduciary.
- **Structure:** Solid investment and engineering infrastructure for investment activation.
- **Sustainability:** Capability of the investment to generate ongoing, meaningful returns and enduring benefit to the growth and development of the travel & tourism sector.
- **Safety:** The safety of the environment from a purely human perspective, ensuring risk-free presence of the people behind the investment working in the destination as temporary residents and/or visitors.
- **Sensibility:** The philosophy and principles of the government and business community of the destination into which investment is being made.
- **Spirit:** The overall energy and outlook towards the future of the people of the destination.
- **Scissors:** The ability to cut through red tape in order to effectively and efficiently mobilise investment programmes.
- **Support:** The willingness demonstrated by the government to embrace investors as partners in the advancement of the destination, assisting investors wherever possible to activate and maximise their investment.

As the global economy recovers, so too will global investment. The travel & tourism sector and the tourism economy deserve a great deal of credit for the impact they have on the advancement of nations.

Now, more than ever, governments and the business community of destinations play a critical role in successfully gaining credit due to

attracting and activating investment into their travel & tourism sector.

For investors, investment into the sector will return to being highly appealing and highly inspiring for investors as markets strengthen in confidence. This appeal strengthens when considering all of the feel-good factors alongside the social, political and economic impact of sector growth.

But investment cannot be at any cost.

PART 2
UP CLOSE

Having looked at the travel & tourism sector from an aerial perspective it is now time to change the lens from wide-angle to zoom, taking a closer look at what it takes to make the sector truly 'work'.

While there are a myriad of dimensions involved in effective, efficient and sustainable tourism sector development, it is also important to look closely at the critical micro aspects which enable a destination to function. This functionality is at a practical level, as well as a competitive economy and as a connected society, all year round.

PART 2 focuses on the WHAT and the HOW, zooming in on ways in which a destination can achieve meaningful differentiation and development.

Do all aspects apply to all destinations? Absolutely not. The old adage remains true: do a few things, and do them well.

As in PART 1, more questions will be asked as a prelude to unlocking solutions which will truly work for the destination, enabling equitable, sustainable destination growth and competitiveness.

Still, as much as the lens is close up, the long-term impact of each action will remain in focus, conscious and cautious of the fact that decisions will have a direct, enduring effect on the destination, its tourism economy and its people.

CHAPTER 6

THE BEAUTY OF THE BRAND

"Why can't we just stay home?" Paula asked, not even looking up from her laptop, her fingers clicking away at e-mails in her usual after-dinner ritual. Hong Kong was now awake, messages already coming in, chiming to attract her attention.

"Really, there's plenty of work to do in the garden. We can go see some movies, maybe do some hiking. I can finally get to all those books sitting on my bedside table. And how about this, I can cook dinner for you every night for a change! There's plenty we can do at home. We don't really need to go away for the holidays."

It was the offer, the threat, to make dinner every night that made Garrett stop what he was doing, put down the washing-up sponge, and move closer to where his wife was sitting at the dining table surrounded by placemats and periodicals.

"Sweetheart, you need to get away. You know it. I know it."

It had been an extremely challenging year. Especially for investment bankers. Since the first rumblings of the global crisis started, things had become incredibly pressurised for Paula. Never before had something like this occurred. There was no way of knowing how long this was going to last, how bad this was going to get, and how many of them would actually make it through. Clients needed reassurance, partners needed results. It was exhausting. She was exhausted. But the work endless. Even now with signs of turn-around starting to appear.

Still, he was absolutely right. She needed to switch off before her batteries wore out. And admittedly before she wore out his understanding.

But if she was going to go away it needed to be somewhere where she really could recharge, her way. No busyness, no markets, no big hotels, no bright lights and big cities. She needed to be still. She needed a place where she could feel herself again. A place where she could give herself one hundred percent to him.

"One hundred percent. One hundred percent." The words kept repeating over and over in her mind, reminding her of something she had seen a short time ago in a magazine when she was flying to somewhere on business. No idea where, there had been too many trips back and forth between Brussels and Asia for her to keep track of. But she was certain it was in a magazine on the flight as that is the only time she seemed to have to pick up the glossies.

With a quick flip of the screen she opened up her browser and keyed the words into the search bar.

"100% PURE NEW ZEALAND"

There it was. The feeling was clear. The promise was clear. The difference was clear. The decision was clear.

"Sweetheart," she called out to Garrett who had returned to the kitchen to put on a fresh pot of coffee. "Sweetheart, I have an idea and I am one hundred percent sure you are going to love it..."

Destination branding has become one of the most exciting, entertaining and expressly competitive aspects of today's tourism industry. Across the world and across the airwaves, television and computer screens are busy carrying music-wrapped images of sand, sea and sunshine, snow-white ski slopes and statuesque monuments, sprawling green landscapes, stunning sunsets, perfect starlit nights and warm smiling faces, all tempting hopeful travellers with the promise of a perfect, personal escape.

Each of these different destination promises comes neatly, sensually packaged in the destination brand. Or at least they try to.

For any destination, central to tourism sector growth is the establishment of a creative, compelling, competitive identity that accurately reflects the experience promise and delivery capability of the destination. Governments around the globe are confidently and proudly investing billions of national revenues each year into establishing destination brand exposure and appeal. With such widespread competition, destination brand advertising on local, regional and international networks has, in many ways, evolved tourism communication to destination pageantry.

Still, for all of the excitement and expectation generated by destination brands, it is vital to not lose focus on the fundamental role and purpose of the brand.

A destination brand, often misunderstood as a logo creatively stating the name of the destination, is in fact an important strategic symbol for the destination. One seemingly simple design is, in fact, a vital reflection and framework of a destination's character, competitive identity and strategy. The fonts selected, colours used, textures employed, creative devices introduced to support the destination name, even the musical arrangements, all work together to reflect specific key elements of the spirit and character of the destination.

A clear set of practical, meaningful tourism objectives and aspirations lie behind a brand's unique features.

Through its presence, the brand showcases the destination to the world, making the desired connection with target audiences.

Ultimately the destination brand seeks to speak to two priority audiences:

- the Traveller, and
- the People of the Destination.

Firstly, the *Traveller.*
For tourists, the destination brand acts as a source of identification of more than just the destination name. It is a reflection of the destination's character and a promise of the traveller experience – the beauty and intrigue of places to be seen, the cultural pageantry of people to be met, the range of local activity to become a part of, the spirit of the destination to be felt. The destination brand acts as both an invitation to the destination and an encapsulation of the unique experiences that the tourists can come 'touch' for themselves.

Secondly, and as importantly, the *People of the Destination.*
This critical target audience is, in fact, composed of a wide range of people. Whether directly or indirectly involved in the tourism industry, the people of the destination, by the very nature of their being emotionally invested in the destination, must feel a connection to the brand. Whether or not their livelihoods are linked to tourism, their lives are. This is their home.

People of the destination include, amongst others:

- local residents,
- diaspora,
- media,
- investors,
- industry stakeholders,
- NGOS,
- academic community, and
- local communities.

For these people the destination brand represents a symbol of the destination's DNA. The destination brand can act as a unifying force, aligning all of the people of the destination behind all that it has to celebrate in its:

- culture,
- spirit,
- personality, and
- future aspirations.

The destination brand must therefore work to unite and inspire the people of the destination to proudly serve in their own way as hosts of visitors to their destination.

Be they formally a part of the tourism industry or simply because they call the destination 'home'.

Ultimately, the brand acts as the **VOICE** of the nation – a vital source of destination identity and messaging for the destination.

With the global tourism industry becoming more and more competitive, crowded and creative, destination brands must achieve clear, confident, meaningful differentiation.

This requires thoughtful, responsible commitment to destination brand development.

As a framework for brand development (and examination), a truly powerful destination brand focuses on the fundamentals of its VOICE:

- **V – Vision:** A powerful destination brand reflects the spirit and aspirations of the people of the destination. It expresses the energy and personality of the destination, proactively shaping its social, cultural, natural and economic destiny. Destinations defining themselves purely by growth should naturally project an energy that confidently expresses the destination's goals and sense of belief in their dreams becoming a proud reality. Destinations rich in history, culture and tradition can effectively showcase and celebrate these features as pillars of the brand's positioning and personality that inspire the future of the destination. The destination brand should project clarity of self-understanding of where the destination has come from and where it is going, acting as a source of traveller excitement and motivation to visit.

  Abu Dhabi's *'Travellers Welcome'* campaign, launched in 2007, provides audiences with an unexpected, inspiring look at how the destination lives its core value of *respect* through its masterful fusion of historical roots and the future vision, tradition and modernity, inviting travellers to share the experience of the emirate.

  Ultimately, the brand should seek to extend an invitation to not just see what travellers are wishing to experience for themselves, but also to discover beyond their expectations of experiences

- **O – Originality**: The destination brand must clearly, confidently and competitively tell a unique, authentic, compelling story about the destination. Creativity is critical. But beware creativity for creativity's sake. The creative expression of the brand acts as a mirror of the creative spirit of the destination itself.

  Importantly, having established the brand's positioning, core messages and look and feel, it is critical to ensure consistency of messaging. A brand is a symbol of identification, understanding and trust. While creative expression of the brand may, and should, change over time, it is important to ensure that brand governance is applied towards the destination brand's DNA – its iconography, look and feel, strategic pillars, pay-off.

  Constant change of, or to, the brand's DNA can result in target audience confusion, distrust of the promise being put forward in communication, and abandonment of interest in the destination.

- **I – Icons:** Each and every destination is leveraging and creating highly memorable, ownable and inspiring symbols uniquely associated with the destination. These can include:
    - – natural environments,
    - – structures,
    - – people,
    - – wildlife,
    - – sport, and
    - – elements of arts and culture.

Destination icons reflect the energy, possibility and pride of the nation. Anchoring the destination brand in icons enables the destination to 'own' truly unique elements of interest and attraction. Focus should be limited to few icons. Destination branding is not a form of cataloguing the full range of experiences open to the traveller.

South Africa's award winning *'Impossible. It's Possible'* campaign, first launched in 2004, utilised its iconic places and personalities to showcase to the world the New South Africa. Importantly, the campaign incorporated the spirit of the new nation to bring its message to life with intensity of meaning and powerful emotional effect.

- **C – Competitiveness:** Importantly, a destination brand must be able to creatively, powerfully, positively and quickly grab the interest of travellers. Competitiveness of brand identity is critical to overall destination competitiveness on the global tourism map.

To truly stand out and achieve recognition, differentiation and interest, creative thought is required not just in the expression of the brand's identity and core messaging, but also in the media mix that is used to achieve desired brand exposure. Strategic thought is required to ensure that the *right messages* are being sent out to the *right people* in the *right media* at the *right time*... and, importantly, with the desired impact.

Destination advertising clutter is a reality of the tourism sector, globally, with little chance that it will subside. Creativity in media execution is as important as creativity in brand expression to ensure that the destination brand's voice is heard as powerfully, meaningfully and purely as possible.

A word of caution:
In an attempt to break through advertising clutter and destination competition, the quest for brand creativity can cross the line. This can occur when:

- creativity turns into clever for clever's sake, and/or
- creative concepts are unable to cross borders.

Sadly, an example of a destination being stung on both accounts is Australia with its 2006 *'So Where the Bloody Hell Are You?'* campaign.

Strategically, it made complete creative sense: The destination brand is forward thinking, warm and engaging. The advertising showcased experiences down under. And it clearly expressed invitation, doing so using local expressions, reflecting local culture and pride. Tick, tick, tick across the boxes.

So why the massive X that was put on the campaign? Why was the campaign banned in the UK, Japan, Canada and the Middle East?

Language. There was no bloody way (pardon the expression) the word 'bloody' was going to be approved for use in advertising in the UK and other markets. And Canada sure as hell was not going to approve the use of the word 'hell'.

Many would argue the PR storm surrounding the campaign was worth it. Five years on it continues to be used as a case study. Surely this is a good thing for the brand?

No.

When it comes to destination brands, not all PR is good PR. Australia suffered an expensive lesson with their campaign error, costing the destination in both campaign investment and brand equity.

At the end of the day it is better to bite one's tongue than risk being tongue-in-cheek.

- **E – Experiential:** Travel today is no longer simply about *seeing* and *doing*; it has become about *feeling*. Destinations that simply showcase static features of destination – places, sights, structures – risk failing to reach out and make an emotional connection with the traveller.

A destination brand which authentically and meaningfully showcases the rich opportunities for engagement of travellers with the destination – *its people, its culture, its places, its nature* – seeds the development of a relationship between the destination and the traveller. Emphasis on select experiences reflecting the pillars of the brand strategy allows the destination to unlock a connection with travellers, pre-, during and post-travel.

Spain's 2010 campaign, *'I Need Spain'*, achieved a break-through by putting the spotlight on the traveller during a time when emotional strain caused by the global recession was increasing people's need to get away, to escape the pressure. Focusing on travellers' need to take a holiday, reconnecting with their family, with their friends, with themselves, TURESPAÑA used an array of Spanish soundbytes as a way of reminding audiences of what they needed, where they needed to be, and what they needed to be doing.

The power of a destination brand is clearly within its VOICE.

Destination brand communicating with a clear, confident, consistent voice opens them up to a world of possibility in growth, development, appreciation, competitive edge and, importantly, pride.

A destination brand is as important to a nation as a name is to a person. It must stay true to its DNA to stay connected to its audiences.

CHAPTER 7

THE POWER OF PPP – PUBLIC-PRIVATE PARTNERSHIPS

As soon as the Minister entered the suite where the reception was being held, Stanley reached for a second glass. Merlot. Having just arrived in from a long day of cabinet meetings and budget debates he looked like he would appreciate a good glass of Merlot. Especially with today's cold rain still pouring down outside, showing no signs of dry relief.

In a gingerly yet targeted fashion, Stanley eased his way towards the fireplace where the Minister was being greeted by the hosts for the evening. Great function room. The crowd seemed interested. And interesting. These business networking sessions are always very interesting. As many agendas as there are people.

"Minister, for you", Stanley said in a low voice, respectfully offering the glass of rich, locally produced yet internationally award-winning red.

"Lovely choice, thank you" the Minister replied in an official tone. And then he paused and looked at Stanley with a smile which friends share. "Actually, this seems a fitting opportunity to finally toast our partnership, Stanley. To the learners!"

"Indeed, Sir. To the learners, Sir. Thank you."

"You know the only way this was going to work, Stanley, was by coming together. Let's just hope others will see this as an example and not an exception."

It was hard to believe that this process had taken almost three years. But in the end clearly it was worth it. The Tourism Academy was finally up and running. The industry had been in desperate need of qualified people to not only build tourism as a service culture today, but build tomorrow's leaders of tourism. But there were just not enough good people. Sure, there are thousands, millions, needing jobs. But tourism was beyond what young people understood it to be. It felt as though there was no motivation for young people to create futures in tourism because they could not grasp what a tourism future looked like for them. Clearly, if the industry was to grow, tourism needed to be understood by young people choosing their professions as tourism Inc. Which meant business skills, communication, finance, leadership, entrepreneurial courage, creativity, people development. The list went on and on.

But as long as tourism was just seen to be about beaches, bikinis and summer jobs bartending, the industry did not stand a chance. As a hotelier Stanley was acutely aware of the number of training and mentorship programmes which were created to try to shift the baseline and raise the level of quality across the industry. Still, individual efforts were not enough, even when combined. Something had to be done on a larger, more sustainable scale, and with huge investment. There was no way around it.

And so Stanley tried to do what everyone around him said cannot be done – get government to pay for it. The budgets were there, surely, considering the way in which the politicians all speak about how important tourism is to the economy. Including jobs. But how long would it take to make it happen? How much time and energy would it take? Was it worth the frustration?

Actually, could the industry afford NOT to do it?

Finally, not sure of the outcome, Stanley put the call through to meet the new Minister of Tourism. Little did he know that government had the same concerns around the future of the industry, and wanted to do something, but did not know how best to get conversation going with the private sector.

In the end, following months of sharing perspective, working through plans and respective positions, undertaking round after round of stakeholder engagement, what finally brought it all together was what the Minister referred to as a PPP, a Public-Private Partnership. As he described it, it made perfect sense: government and private business partner on a project to deliver an outcome which satisfies both of their objectives and leverages their respective strengths.

In this case, for government it meant creating an academic institution which developed the skills and job opportunities for learners at college level wanting to work and grow in tourism with the reassurance of having a degree behind their names. For business it meant creating a single, rigorous curriculum and set of performance standards which developed an ongoing flow of qualified, committed and inspired people ready to work in the tourism industry.

Amazing, actually. All it took was three little letters, PPP, and three years. In hindsight it was no time at all. What are three years when you are building the future for the next generation?

Within any tourism economy there are, naturally, two powerful forces: the Public Sector and the Private Sector. These two forces have the ability to achieve greatness.

The Public Sector, that being government acts as the architect of a nation's core identity, policy and legacy. With a clear mandate of national growth and development, efforts and energies of officials and institutions seek to advance society, the economy and the environment for the well-being of all people – present and future. In theory, visions are defined, policies are developed, programmes are created, metrics (especially as regards employment, opportunity creation and national competitiveness) are defined, budgets are allocated, outcomes are anticipated. Timelines can stretch beyond tenure. Success is generally defined qualitatively. Design is everything.

The Private Sector, effectively the business community, shares the desire for future growth and development of the nation, however with a different set of goals, metrics, expectations and end accountabilities. With firm business plans, objectives, investment allocations, accountabilities and targets for returns, success is generally defined quantitatively. Delivery is everything.

Working independently, which is most often the case, the Public and Private sectors are each able to mobilise their respective strengths, scale and sensibilities to have an enduring, positive impact on a destination. Each trying to establish and advance the tourism economy, the sectors apply resources towards initiatives that, from each of their points of view, are critical to long-term quality and competitiveness of the destination. In theory, they are united by a common goal of tourism development, with a shared sense of vision and commitment to realisation of same. In theory.

More often than not, however, these forces are in opposition. Differing priorities, timelines and processes result in differences of opinion which cause different paths to be taken.

The net effect: underutilisation of critical resources, underappreciation of respective contributions to industry development and under-achievement of destination potential.

The fact remains, if these two forces were to come together, working synergistically for development of the tourism economy in a way that truly leveraged their respective areas of experience and expertise, the value could be exponential.

Fortunately there is a way to make this happen: it's about the power of PPPs – Public-Private Partnerships.

Recognising the importance and innate logic of bringing government and private enterprise together, yet the challenges, a vehicle was created by government to bring together the public and private sector entities, from any economic sector, for the achievement of shared objectives.

PPPS have become a globally utilised term and template for the establishment and execution of projects that call upon co-operation between government and private business. Effectively a contract between government and private business, a PPP makes it possible for two traditionally opposing forces to come together as experts, combining:

- visions,
- goals,
- access,
- structures,
- expertise,
- intelligence,
- funds, and
- people resources

for the sole purpose of achievement of a clearly defined, mutually desired end-goal.

Importantly, PPPS are activated when specific challenges need to be addressed, or opportunities need to be unlocked, which clearly require the support of both parties.

These may include:

Government's need for:

- specific skills or expertise for implementation,
- capital investment,
- risk management,
- accelerated delivery,
- budget leverage, and
- industry advancement.

And/or:

Private business's need for:

- planning permission,
- incentives,
- funding,
- policy modification,
- lobbying support, and
- elimination of red tape.

The PPP tightly outlines the fundamentals of an initiative so that both partners are able to deliver against set expectations as mutually understood, mutually agreed and mutually invested.

From a tourism perspective, PPPs are developed to directly address destination needs including:

- infrastructure development,
- safety and security systems,
- regional development,
- crisis recovery,
- economic stimulation or recovery,
- education/skills development,
- mega-event activation, and
- marketing and promotion of the destination,

and a variety of other destination-specific needs.

Most recently PPPs were strongly encouraged by the UNWTO as a vehicle for stimulating tourism sector recovery during the 2008/9 global economic crisis. The global recession which caused a dramatic arresting of industry growth rates experienced prior to Q4 of 2008 generated sharp losses in the global tourism economy, employment and revenues in particular. PPP formed an important lever for governments to respark industry activity and support with private sector stakeholders.

Interestingly, what one party may see as a simple project, the other may see as a profoundly important programme.

One such example of a PPP which created an impact far exceeding expectations was a seemingly simple road infrastructure development which brought the provincial government and a private hotelier together. *Bushmans Kloof Wilderness Reserve and Wellness Retreat* in South Africa, a globally award winning property of the Red Carnation Collection nestled in the Cederberg Mountains, faced ongoing challenges in resort development due to guests being forced to travel a 50 km stretch of road known as Pakhuis Pass which, during times of rain and resulting erosion, severely hampered journey safety, duration and comfort. Through discussions and PPP development with local government and the neighbouring community, tarring of the road was undertaken.

The effect was transformational. Not only were resort guests able to dramatically decrease travel time and increase journey pleasure, as stated by Alan Winde, Minister of Tourism, Finance and Economic Development, Provincial Government of the Western Cape:

> *"In Clanwilliam, the simple act of tarring a stretch of road to Bushmans Kloof has unlocked economic and tourism activity to the area, and enhanced the quality of life for local communities. PPPs of this nature have proven to not just impact development of the T&T sector. Indeed, they have become an essential mechanism to drive employment and economic growth on a much larger scale."*

Ultimately, as with any partnership, commitment and accountability to delivery are paramount.

That said, while a seemingly simple concept with logical rationale, PPPs represent so much more than simply a partnership between the public and private sector. They are the platform for possibility.

It is therefore strongly recommended that when tourism industry projects are being examined for viability, whatever their size and scale, the lens of PPPs should be carefully looked through.

Before final go/no go decisions are made, tourism leaders, within both the public and private sectors, would benefit greatly from asking themselves the following questions:

- Does this project support the greater destination growth plan?
- What are the key success factors for project delivery: financial, social, psychological?
- What resources are available to ensure delivery?
- What barriers to delivery exist? Funds? Skills? Access? Time?
- Have the right stakeholders been brought on board?
- What role should government play, if at all?
- What role should the private sector play, if at all?
- Would creation of a PPP strengthen probability of successful delivery?

To truly deliver PPPs must represent shared PURPOSE, PASSION and PRINCIPLES.

Period.

CHAPTER 8

GOING GREEN – COMMITMENT BEYOND THE COLOUR

She wished someone could explain it to her. Surely somehow it made sense. Surely. This was supposed to be a conference on Greening Tourism, on establishing a green economy. Everyone knew this was important. It is no longer about inconvenience – it is about inescapable, immediate responsibility. And so a region's worth of tourism industry stakeholders had come together in this beautiful, blessed little corner of Vietnam to discuss how, together, the region moves forward in establishing and embedding a green approach to tourism planning and promotion.

From across government and the private sector, NGOs, academia and media, over two hundred people had gathered. Very impressive, indeed. Clearly there was recognition that for the island nations of Asia to go green they needed to get together and get going. Made complete sense.

But sitting here, freezing in the over-air-conditioned conference room, looking out at tables covered in paper, Sunita could not help but shake her head. It just did not make sense. Surely she was not the only one to feel a sense of hypocrisy. There was no need to make the conference room so cold. Even in summer in Asia. It was freezing in there! And why was it necessary for delegates to use this event as a way of throwing a blanket of destination and tour company brochures, newsletters and CDs over the meeting desks. Tonight the cleaning staff for the conference are going to have to clear away at least seventy percent of all the 'stuff' that is left behind by delegates who simply do not have the interest or luggage space for all the extra paper. Surely attendees are wondering why we are so openly in violation of our original objectives. Surely!

The irony is that to turn up the temperature of the room, even by just two to three degrees, would save the venue money, increasing revenues for hosting the event. And attention of participants would increase as the chill felt would not distract from discussions underway.

It was at that moment that Sunita realised that the true gauge of success in 'going green' on one's actions is not one's scorecard or calculation of carbon footprint. These are metrics. Important, but not the inspiration for change. The start is in fact one's conscience. She knew then what she was doing was wasteful. Whether it is leaving lights on, throwing away bags, turning the a/c up too high, not incorporating grey water into building plans, not ensuring solar panels and timed lighting are engineered into hotel designs. There's that little inner pang of guilt. And the stronger it gets, the more one needs to put a voice to it. To put a stop to the waste.

And so as the delegates all took their seats and the Programme Director took the microphone to welcome the audience back from lunch, she raised her hand: "Please, Programme Director, may I request..."

Since the turn of the century, the colour green has taken on a whole new meaning. Many years before *'Going Green'* first became a familiar expression, effectively back in the 1980s and 1990s, the colour green was a reflection of the choice to be a part of a niche culture, one which actively supported a more eco-friendly way of life. Green implied greater natural texture of life, more aware of and sensitive to the impact of one's lifestyle choices. The concept of being Green touched the spirits and lifestyles of those who sought to live on Earth in a more earthy way. And when travelling, journeys were to places less known, less accessible, more at risk of extinction, more open to learning about the value of living. It was a statement, one which progressed to even becoming a fashion statement.

The arrival of the year 2000 brought with it a profound shift in how the world understood its connections. And then in 2006, with the growth in global awareness of a truly inconvenient truth, a green wave of consciousness spread across the globe.

Since then the concept of green has evolved from being about *fashionability* to being about *responsibility*. More and more the colour green has spread, from products and packaging to attitudes and actions.

Slowly, scientific and sincere awareness and acceptance of the impact of each and every individual on the world has been occurring.

Today the colour green has soaked into the hearts and minds of people across all countries, all cultures, all sensibilities. The need to do things right to be able to do the right thing has gone mainstream. Thankfully.

This is especially true within the travel & tourism community, a global community committed to showcasing the beauty of the world through all that nature, culture and spirit has to offer, that has for years recognised the importance of treading lightly across the world's array of destinations, leaving only footprints.

The dramatic growth of the sector has caused a clash of colour. As hundreds of millions of travellers cross borders each year, the temptation for increased amounts of bankable green – revenues generated from visitor receipts – can lead to decision-making around sector development which decreases amounts of natural green. Yet the number of green tourism campaigns increases, some genuine, some simply green-washing, all impacting brand and sector credibility.

Before jumping into the green section of the creative agency's colour spectrum, and creating promotions declaring *'being green'*, it is critical for tourism government bodies and businesses to take a close look at what exactly going green means for the destination strategically, philosophically, operationally and economically... not just creatively.

And how genuine their intentions and commitment are to long-term growth.

The definitions and dimensions of green are many. While wording may differ depending on the source, the spirit is, by and large, the same. The breadth and depth of opportunity for a destination to adopt a green philosophy, and go on to establish genuine green credentials, is immense. There are a number of ways in which a destination can work with the environment to create a unique, compelling, competitive destination.

These can include, to name but a few:

- **Eco-tourism:** One of the most presenceful and popular approaches to going green, eco-tourism is a globally recognised and celebrated niche offering which puts engaging with the natural environment of the destination at the centre of the offering. Destinations which pride themselves in abundant wildlife, flora and fauna have successfully created traveller experiences which make it possible to be immersed in and involved with nature as a tourism attraction which can be seen, felt and even contributed towards.

In addition, eco-tourism destinations offer the benefit of an enhanced sense of wellness from being in such a 'pure' environment (even if sophisticated in design, as is found in Six Senses Wellness Resorts across the world) with opportunity to partake in excursions focused on being at one with nature here and now.

Interestingly, eco-tourism is also becoming a means of directing destination growth, and dispersion of benefits, in areas at risk of tourism industry overdevelopment.

As explained by Eco-tourism Society Pakistan (ESP): *"Eco-tourism is a travel activity that ensures direct financial support to local people where tourism activities are being generated and enjoyed. It teaches travellers to respect local cultures (and environments) of destinations where travellers are visiting. It supports small stakeholders to ensure money must not go out from the local economies. It discourages mass construction of hotels, tourism resorts and mass activities in fragile areas."*[4]

Across the globe, destinations as differing in local culture as Costa Rica, Madagascar, Nepal and Ecuador are remarkably similar in their dependence on eco-tourism as a means of building their economies and environments, in tandem, for the long term.

- **Eco-friendly:** Destinations which define themselves as *going green* from an *eco-friendly* perspective openly and voluntarily adopt and express environmentally-friendly practices which, while seemingly small, can in fact make a big difference when added up. The desire to be considerate of the impact of the industry (or parts of it) on the environment is there, with efforts made to do the little things which are simply the right thing to do. Eco-friendly efforts include basic environmentally-considerate changes to existing infrastructure, ie. frequency of linen washing, keypads in hotel rooms to turn on/off power mains, adjusted air-conditioner temperatures in large spaces, replacement of incandescent light bulbs to energy-saving bulbs, selective recycling efforts (ie. grey water). Interestingly, destinations venturing into these practices even incrementally will notice a positive impact on the bottom line.

As effectively a choice, eco-friendly can be expressed as *eco-lite.*

- **Eco-policies:** Getting more serious about the impact which the industry has on the environment, enforcement of eco-policies by governments and tourism corporations reflects the fundamental philosophy held by leaders of a destination and tourism business towards energy conservation and environmental responsibility. Enforcement of policy removes the window of choice for members of the tourism community, making changes to existing and future tourism products and services (ie. changes to increase energy efficiency, and/or reduce wastage of resources) a must.

These policies do not apply purely to destinations that exist within locations surrounded by greenery and teeming with wildlife. Even the most built-up, uber-urban, heavily populated areas which could be described more as concrete jungles than even garden cities can successfully impose and activate green policies and incentives. Macau, as an example, has put in place a green hotel awards programme for international developers of resorts and casinos scrambling to get a piece of the action and place a bet on tourism growth in the new Asian tourism hot spot which also proudly holds UNESCO World Heritage status. The initiative by Macau's Environment Council (now Environmental Protection Bureau), which was introduced in 2007, drives the importance of environmental management in the hotel sector across the industry while giving high profile, highly respected recognition to those hotels mobilising environmentally-sound management policies.

- **Eco-engineered:** Linked to policy, eco-engineering is the adoption of new generation technology and practices into new tourism products, services and developments, effectively making obsolete old, less energy-efficient methods. This increasing sensitivity to the design and development of tourism industry assets, particularly major structures such as airports, retail centres, theatres, hotels and conference centres, can have a dramatic effect on the impact of the industry on the environment, visibly and invisibly.

  The following eco-engineering concepts are just a few of the energy-smart and environmentally-sensitive techniques increasingly being built into new tourism infrastructure:

  – Water heating: Heat recovered from the hotel's air-conditioning system used to warm water for swimming pools; solar panels for water used in hotels and spas.
  – Temperature control: Solar glazing in windows and doors assists in maintaining constant interior temperatures.

– Lighting: Energy-efficient lights and lamps; movement sensors for after-hour lighting in common areas and underground parking; keycard room power control.
– Air-conditioning: Sensors automatically switch off air-conditioning in the bedrooms when doors to balconies or terraces are opened.
– Irrigation: Rainwater directed off the roofs via an extensive underground pipe network to a large storage tank for use in the gardens.

Interestingly, initial investment into green design very soon proves to be a valuable revenue protector as operating costs can be dramatically reduced.

The green economy is a reality, a much needed and a deeply meaningful one. Taking into account the above possible approaches to going green, and many others which exist, tourism industry leaders within both the public and private sector need to look closely at how they plan to, and often must, incorporate going green into their tourism growth strategy, ethos, brand and business models. Form follows function. Function follows philosophy.

To be green, truly green, is not about posting messages to reuse hotel towels and making corporate statements about being enviro-conscious. It is about making a commitment to making a positive difference by letting one's conscience guide every moment in decision-making when delivering and further developing the traveller experience.

Before positioning and profiling the destination as being green at heart, the following questions need to be answered, honestly, by tourism leaders:

- Is this a genuine, long-term commitment to change the way things are done?
- Is there a willingness and readiness to invest, ongoing, in necessary conversions of systems and approaches?
- Does consistency in green philosophy and practices exist through all aspects of the offering(s), or is it limited to only certain areas?
- Is the philosophy of going green understood and lived by all people of the destination/organisation?

- Are the right measures and monitoring systems in place to ensure achievement of, and ongoing improvement on, green targets?
- How does this fit in with our brand messages?
- Have the criteria for future projects and programmes been defined to ensure compliance with green standards?
- Do stakeholders and partners genuinely share a commitment to destination/business growth through green?

Green consciousness is a compass for waste and risk detection, opportunity and responsibility. Ultimately, going green is not only good for the environment; it is good for the brand and good for business.

Commitment to green within the tourism sector goes far deeper than commitment to a colour and a campaign. It is a commitment to responsible leadership of the destination and the global tourism sector per se: environmentally, socially, culturally and economically – naturally.

CHAPTER 9

THE SERIOUS BUSINESS OF BUSINESS TOURISM

As soon as the e-mail arrived into his inbox Chris opened it. The others could wait. It had been two long, hard years of challenges, not problems but challenges, in his business, and finally there was a sense of restored confidence.

Like so many others, the economic downturn had put his business not into a financial crisis, but a crisis of morale. And it was hurting not just the company's bottom line, but the company's culture. This place which he built, over all these years, his life's work, always meant something. There was a pride and sense of purpose, for the now hundreds of people who work for him. He knew them all – their names, their roles, their backgrounds, and in many cases their families. But these past months had turned the company's purpose to survival. It was scary. He had to protect what he had built. Even today his people never really knew how severe it was. Customers were simply not buying.

And so he pulled back on spending. There was nothing else he could do – he had to cut budgets. He had to cut the parties, and the incentive trips and the business travel. He wasn't just trying to save money, he was trying to save jobs. People's livelihoods were on the line. Everyone felt it across the company.

Looking at the e-mail he felt a sense of relief. The annual Sales and Marketing conference date had been set. After two years of having to cancel the one event which brings all of his customer-focused employees together from across the country, this year they were going ahead with it.

It was the right thing to do, no question about it. He knew how desperately his business needed it. These people were the front line of the business. They needed to find new and better ways of doing things, sharing ideas around how to get customers buying again, and how to keep costs at a minimum without risking results. It would also be very healthy for the business culture. His people needed focus and faith back again.

He chose a great venue. The Board of Directors was a bit surprised – they had assumed it was going to be a city hotel. But he knew that the place mattered. It was going to be a resort, a venue where everyone could feel away from it all, using the time and space to let their imaginations open up again.

It wasn't about partying and golf and all recreation. The down-time was unquestionably important but that was not why he was taking them all away, over 150 of his team. It was for the opportunities for business growth that come from some of the sharpest minds of his business getting together and getting back to business.

Click. e-Invitation accepted!

The 2008/9 global economic downturn put significant pressure on the ability for people to travel for both work and play. The global travel & tourism industry saw a severe falling off in critical metrics. The world was grounded. As a result, the tourism economies of destinations across the globe felt the pain.

Travellers, needing to get away from the stresses and fears of the recession, had to turn to their computer screens to enjoy some travel escapism through the *'I wish'* travel planning process. Flight search engines, destination websites and other travel pages increased in their wishful traveller audiences. Sun seekers turned to sun.coms and sun beds for maybe-one-day destination planning. And business people turned away from their corporate travel agents and turn on Skype and other video-conferencing technology to keep connected to key contacts across the country and world.

Business travel experienced a particular bruising in 2009. From small to large, businesses across the globe needing to manage costs had to, since the beginning of the open usage of the R-word (Recession), looked to travel budgets to find fat that could be trimmed. Meetings, conferences, conventions and incentive trips were cancelled. The entire MICE industry (Meetings, Incentives, Conferences and Exhibitions) effectively shut down. There was no reason to celebrate, no reason to convene, no budget to incentivise. Banks were collapsing, businesses were closing and headcounts were being cut.

Even more painful, reputations were being ruined. Businesses seen to be conferencing were being openly accused (and often publicly shamed) for irresponsible spending on perks and parties when there were serious issues to deal with at the bottom line. The trips and tee-times and spa treatments had to stop, the politicians declared. Those days were over. Gratitude had to shift from annual get-aways to daily employment.

Most notably, an unfortunate comment made by President Obama in early 2009 condemning excessive spending on conferences when the government had to approve federal bailout. *"You can't get corporate jets, you can't go take a trip to Las Vegas or go down to the Super Bowl on the taxpayer's dime,"* the President declared.[5]

Las Vegas, a city known for overnight fortunes, saw millions lost in conference bookings disappear by dawn, with thousands of tourism employees fearing for their jobs. A minimum of three major banks cancelled meetings in Las Vegas to avoid association and criticism. Tourism officials estimate cancellations due to the fear of visibility cost the region's tourism-related businesses in excess of $132 million. This in a destination responsible for one million jobs.

Fortunately, a silver lining did appear. Courageous, clear and quick thinking on the part of USTA turned a desperate situation into a learning opportunity for the new administration in Washington and the people of the USA. The creation of a national campaign clearly communicating the importance of the tourism economy to the nation, and value of business tourism, raised the priority of the sector in the eyes and policies of national leadership.

Still, a dark cloud hung over the global business tourism sector. Even those businesses willing and able to spend on large scale business events were forced to cut back on their plans purely to keep corporate images lean and clean. Hotel rooms, empty. Banquet halls, empty. Conference rooms, empty. Plenary sessions, empty. Breakaway rooms, empty. Business centres, empty. Hopes for a return of bookings, empty.

Concerns grew as numbers fell. The business of tourism, a front line business, felt both an emotional and financial crisis. Destinations engineered for the MICE sector, the likes of Las Vegas and Dubai, saw black ink turn to red faster than printer ink cartridges could be replaced.

To this day, as the economic crisis is slowly and cautiously shifting into 'recovery' status in markets around the world, Business Tourism/the MICE sector, remains depressed. Alternatives to business travel have been adopted, especially in terms of video conferencing and webinars. And extras are no longer expected.

There have been significant studies undertaken during the Great Recession of 2008/9 questioning the risks of business development dependent on technology. Particularly at the top. Regardless of how advanced our technology has become, as the need for 3D grows the higher the importance of the decision becomes. Face-to-face is critical. Especially as global business forces cultures of incredible distance and differences to connect. Intuitively we all know this – there is no replacement for direct contact when the issue at hand is important to us.

As revealed by a study conducted by USTA and the Destination Travel Association in 2009[6]:

- For every dollar invested in business travel, companies realise $12.50 in incremental revenue.
- More than half of business travellers stated that 5% – 20% of their company's new customers were the result of trade show participation.
- According to business travellers across all industries, 25% of existing customers and 28% of revenue could be lost to competitors if customers were not met in person.
- Executives stated that in order to achieve the same effect of incentive travel, an employee's total base compensation would need to be increased by 8.5%.

Going from 100% to 0% business travel activity is not an option. There has to be a point of correction, the position on the scale where the right balance is found between investment and expected impact.

Because the fact is this:

When people meet, when they talk, when they share ideas and when they create, opportunities and energy and excitement bubble up.

An excellent example of business tourism opportunity turned into action can be found down under in Melbourne, Australia. As expressed by Melanie de Souza, General Manager International Marketing, Tourism Victoria, Australia:

> *"Business events are a rapidly growing sector globally and are crucial to Melbourne's tourism industry, providing $1.2 billion per annum to Victoria and 22,000 jobs.*
>
> *From a brand standpoint, significant conferences and conventions consolidate Victoria's impressive reputation of hosting and staging diverse events, including sporting and cultural events, as part of its annual calendar. State of the art tourism and events infrastructure, including its newly completed 6 star green-rated convention centre, places Melbourne in good stead to secure a growing share of this high yield segment.*
>
> *Also, Melbourne's strong business and trade reputation across an array of sectors including, to name a few, medical research, biotechnology and design, naturally complements the city's bid to host business events in related fields. These events offer key local and visiting industry luminaries the opportunity to network, share initiatives and foster innovative partnerships, which in turn boost industry and economic growth."*

With all of this creative energy and growing possibility, solutions are found – solutions which unlock growth, development, economic recovery and black ink.

Business travel has a role to play in economic recovery. A critical role.

There is also the very real, very visible and very audible effect of the convergence of groups of people on a destination for a conference, convention, meeting or incentive event. Hotel reception desks become centres of organised chaos as wide-eyed, well uniformed staff are confronted by excited delegates seeking room keys, conference packs, tour information and currency exchange. At times the day the conference came to town can appear as the day the circus came to town. All the activity, all the running around, all that noise.

The noise reaches even beyond the venues themselves. Related businesses enjoy the benefit as business tourists spend not only around the destination, but are increasingly extending the length of their stays through pre- and post-meeting leisure breaks.

Listening closely, it is clear. All that noise is in fact music. It is the music of people meeting, people working, people moving forward.

The new challenge to the MICE/Business Tourism sector is not simply in rebuilding numbers of bookings, jobs and revenues, it is in rebuilding credibility. And the ownership of that challenge is the industry itself.

Business tourism must step up, reach out, and ensure the message is clear, sharing with the global business community the importance of meetings, conferences and conventions to restimulate thinking, restimulate ideas and restimulate the economy.

It's not about the circus, with all its clowns and chaos. It's not about the aerial acts. It's not about all of the theatrics taking place under the big top. It's about all the possibility that exists within all of that creativity.

We need to get back into the circus tent.

CHAPTER 10

TAKING CARE OF TRAVELLERS

They are so easy to spot. Tourists. There they are, lily white, big bikinis by Rio standards, lying on hotel beach towels trying desperately to soak up Brazil's bronzing sunshine. And beach bags on open display. Bags full of valuables from cameras to passports. Bags kept close for fear of loss to watchful locals with quick hands.

Paulo has been walking these beaches for years. He has seen it all. The hopeful yet watchful tourists, their behaviour revealing their suspicion of anyone from Rio, even though they have come from across the world to be here and relax! Ironic. He cannot help but smile.

And today, even more inspiring of his smile is that he knows how little those tanning tourists need to worry. Because he, a local member of the tourist host programme, along with hundreds of others, is there to subtly watch over tourists, allowing them to shut their eyes and rest while they lie in the sought-after sunshine.

When he heard about this programme, the tourism host programme, he immediately became excited. As a retired policeman he knew all too well the challenges which Rio faced – essentially those which any major city across the globe with pockets of poverty faces.

And he also knew very well how important tourism is to Rio's economy. Without tourists his people cannot find work, cannot make an honest living, cannot take care of their families and cannot live in the shadow of Christ's Monument – a true Wonder of the World and icon of deep pride and meaning for the people of Brazil – in clear conscience.

And so, to be able to play an active part in ensuring tourists are truly cared for by being carefully watched over, is something he sees as a duty. He loves being a member of the Tourism Police force. Because deep down he knows that protecting tourists will make it possible for tourists to appreciate all that Rio has to offer. He is caringly watching over them.

It will also let locals planning to misbehave know that he is also watching them, so they must not even try to cause trouble! The people of Rio must take pride in their city as a leading destination for travellers of the world. The more tourists that come, the more Rio will grow, peacefully. More peace, more pride. More pride, more peace. And more tourists. That, Paulo thinks to himself, has to have an effect on the spirit of the people of Rio.

With pride, he smiles.

To be a member of the international tourism industry is to accept the responsibility of taking care of travellers. Because traveller safety is everyone's responsibility.

Responsible destination development has, rightly, taken a front row seat in the strategies, policies and philosophies of nations seeking to grow and develop their tourism economies. Building a tourism destination responsibly, actively conscious of the impact which the tourism industry has on the place, people and promise of the destination, is critical to the long-term health and well-being of the destination.

As a result, members of both the public and private sector have begun to come together across the global tourism community to talk sustainability, responsibility, longevity and accountability – fundamentals of sector growth and development.

Principles and programmes are being created which ensure that growth of the destination takes into careful consideration the impact of travellers on:

- the natural environment of the destination,
- the established culture and traditions of the destination,
- the style and character of the destination,
- the spirit and ethos of the people of the destination, and
- the immediate growth and development needs of the destination along with its future aspirations.

The definition of 'Responsible Tourism' has evolved organically to include both the tangibles and the intangibles of the destination, both the present and the future, both the expectations and the experience.

Very importantly, it also reaches out to include both the travel destination and the traveller.

Responsibility for the well-being of the destination is not only the responsibility of the tourism sector – it is also the responsibility of the tourist.

The world has seen such dramatic change since the turn of century. This is particularly true when it comes to the issue of safety and security. With the increased frequency and severity of natural and man-made crises over the past decade, our feeling of safety, both physically and psychologically, has been challenged. And our sense of security less secure.

Sadly, there have been a number of moments when civilisation has failed to appear civilised.

The travel & tourism sector has been particularly bruised at a number of levels. Growing concerns around safety and security of destinations, and the process of getting to them, has caused travellers to rethink *if, where, when* and *how* they travel.

To reflect on a few examples:

- **Natural Disasters:** The devastating tsunami in Asia in 2004, Hurricanes Katrina in New Orleans and Wilma in Mexico in 2005, and more recently the earthquake in Haiti in 2010, have demonstrated over and over the incredible forces of nature. And how they can grab hold of us at any time, in any place, in any form, and with no warning whatsoever. Leaving as much fear in their wake as rubble, not only was there severe damage to the tourism, social and economic infrastructures of these tourism-dependent destinations, but also extensive damage to the psyche of both locals and tourists alike.
- **Health Crisis:** The invisible can often be more concerning than the visible, especially where pandemics are concerned. The outbreak of rare, unexpected and initially unpreventable and untreatable diseases in different parts of the world, and their ability to spread to epidemic and pandemic proportions through passenger air travel, has turned passenger illness into a serious threat to the health of travellers and travel plans.
- **Terrorism:** Even before 9/11, we were conscious of risks of being in the wrong place at the wrong time. But then 9/11 happened, and not only were we reminded of how interconnected our world is, we were awoken to the risks that these interconnections could bring. The global aviation industry in particular immediately clamped down on travel rules, regulations and restrictions in a dramatic, determined attempt to stop trouble in its travelling tracks. Changes introduced into the passenger travel experience from check-in to disembarking are now non-negotiable. The process of travel has become increasingly complicated, drawn out and time consuming.
- **Shutdown of Transport Systems:** 2010 was a year which saw efforts of travel & tourism recovery marred by a series of shutdowns of international air space. It started in April, when the dense, enduring ash cloud which hung above Iceland's

Eyjafjallajokull volcano resulted in close to a week of flight cancellations, leaving tens of thousands of passengers stranded across the globe, unable to get to where they needed to, or get back. Weddings were cancelled as brides (and grooms) could not make it to the altar. Babies were born with fathers offering support via video chat, holiday plans were left to the mercy of supportive tour operators and hoteliers able to adjust bookings. And millions of roses (and resulting export earnings) in Kenya's flower farms limply looked to the skies above as freight planes sat on the runway, grounded. Like *déjà vu*, groundings occurred again, and again, as winter set in, climaxing over the most emotionally charged time of year with travellers warned they might not make it home for the holidays. Billions lost in revenues, and countless tears shed. Without a doubt, it will happen again in some flight-stopping shape or form, making travellers nervous of plans and weighing up probabilities.

- **Crime:** At both individual and collective levels, direct in-destination crime against travellers feels to be increasing. Be it credit card fraud or personal attacks, travellers are ever-conscious of the presence of personal risk. Comfort zones are decreasing, trust levels are decreasing, suspicions are increasing.

Sadly, these realities have cast a heavy shadow over the global travel & tourism playground, industry and opportunity. Accepting fear as a part of a visitor's experience to a destination is not acceptable.

What must never be forgotten by tourism leaders within both the public and private sectors is that when a traveller begins the planning process of travel, they are investing their time, money and energy into an event which they hope will leave them stronger – be it in business, in mind, in spirit, in creativity, in sense of self, whatever the case may be. That hope is pure.

The emotional investment in travel can often far exceed the financial investment.

As a result, once on the path of preparation, purity of mindset can change, and often not for the better. Be it on an individual or collective level, increases in risks on travellers have changed the way the world views and visits nations. Incidents as individual as pick-pocketing or price cheating, and as collective as terror attacks or earth tremors, have travellers looking more suspiciously and skeptically at places in the world which once may have been deemed enticing and inviting.

As strongly as destination marketing and development experts across the globe apply their minds and efforts to attracting travellers, so too should focus be put on protecting travellers by these same industry leaders.

This is not about increasing tourism police forces. For a tourist to arrive into a destination and see voluminous police presence does not extend a sense of safety. Instead it creates a feeling of fear and reason for distrust. A guardian level of police presence is absolutely acceptable as a respectful, respected, responsive presence. But excessive force simply communicates excessive reason for fear.

Instead it is about creating, nurturing, developing, up-skilling and celebrating a tourism culture which appreciates and celebrates visitors, be they business or leisure, all year round.

A critical component of any Destination Growth and Development Strategy is a clear, committed approach to visitor safety and security. This aspect of destination development acts as a vital foundation to destination building and sustainability – as important as infrastructure, policy, governance and marketing investment.

As shared by Christopher Rodrigues CBE, Chairman Visit Britain:

> *"Many small businesses make up the eco-system of a modern tourism industry. Their diversity adds to the rich experiences a nation offers its visitors. Yet some industry challenges must be addressed within a single framework and none is more important than security. While it is widely recognised that travel & tourism enhances understanding between the peoples of the world, this can only be achieved if the industry keeps their care and well-being at the forefront of its activities."*

Safety and security are also aspects of brand equity. A destination which takes seriously taking care of travellers to the destination is a destination which has care, compassion, responsibility and respect as part of its brand DNA.

It is vital that the national Department of Tourism and National Tourism Authority work with all stakeholder partners, especially the:

- Department of Safety and Security,
- Department of Health, and
- Department of Home Affairs,

as well as:

- hotel associations,
- convention and visitor bureaus,
- Chambers of Commerce, and
- airport authorities,

to create the policies, systems and structures needed to ensure travellers are kept safe, and the tourism industry is kept ready and responsive to when things can and do go wrong.

It is natural for travellers to be concerned. Sadly, and with far too much frequency, bad things have been happening.

When natural disaster hits it is common for travellers to ask the following questions:

- *How long will it take for the destination to rebuild?*
- *How can rebuilding take place for the tourism industry without compromising efforts to get the locals back on their feet?*
- *How can a tourist check into a hotel if it could come crashing down if the earth moves again?*
- *How can I lie sunbathing by the seaside if the waters might rise and sweep everyone and everything away again?*

Similarly, when visiting destinations with a reputation for crime, it is natural for travellers to ask the following questions:

- *Is it safe to go out at night?*
- *Is it safe to wear jewellery in public, or carry a camera, or ask for directions, or look at a map?*

And as recent as ten years ago to sneeze would have caused those nearby to spontaneously say "bless you". Today, as H1N1, Bird Flu, SARS and other diseases travel the world, travellers now spontaneously respond to sneezing and coughing with a flinch of fear... 'what ifs?' pass through one's mind.

- *What if the person sneezing has H1N1?*
- *What if I get it?*
- *What if they quarantine me?*
- *What will this do to my holiday/business travel plans?'*

It may in fact not require a sneeze to create these worries. Walking past an airport temperature scanner can have the same reaction... whether one is feeling healthy or not.

Through proactive, collective, consistent, well communicated, clearly expressed and continuous commitment to traveller safety and security, travellers will see *and feel* the safety of a destination. And the tourism community will recognise and accept that success of the industry is directly tied to safety of travellers.

Tourism professionals taking on the honour and responsibility of inviting and hosting travellers to their airlines, destinations, hotels, resorts, attractions and events need to ensure that a readiness exists for the times when, sadly, things go wrong.

While each situation will demand a different scale of response, the fundamental questions which need to be asked, before a situation occurs, are the same:

- *Is it clear who visitors can call in case of an emergency? Is it clear how tourism leaders will be informed and involved if something goes wrong?*
- *Is it clear who is in charge in government? Is it clear who in the business community is the first point of contact?*
- *How can resources be unlocked, quickly, when needed to address urgent needs of travellers in crisis?*
- *Is it clear who will be leading communications, defining and disseminating core messages so all parties involved remain 'on script'?*
- *Is it clear how the stakeholder community needs to be brought together, quickly, to understand and address a crisis?*
- *Is it clear how the media will be engaged, informed and empowered as a partner working with the tourism industry?*

- *Is it clear how all parties involved will be kept updated as the crisis unfolds and is resolved?*
- *Is there a post-event review process to ensure the tourism community learns from what has happened, working to increase effectiveness and efficiency of response the next time a crisis occurs?*

Through genuine, compassionate insight into travellers' fears and risks, and scenario planning around the 'what ifs' a destination can develop policies and practices which proactively, effectively yet very subtly take care of their visitors, *physically and emotionally*.

In so doing a destination builds destination appeal, appreciation and brand equity through building traveller peace of mind.

To fear the unfamiliar is natural. To welcome and embrace strangers as guests is tourism.

CHAPTER 11

NICHE TOURISM – POWERFUL SPARKS FOR 365 TOURISM

Setting the table, carefully placing the cutlery and candlesticks, Maggie was so excited! How long had it been since she last held a dinner party? And set the table herself? This evening was her evening – she had picked the perfect menu, the perfect wines, the perfect desert, the perfect flowers. Why? Because for the first time in years she was feeling perfect! And standing in the doorway watching his wife carefully yet confidently move about the dining room, Brian knew it also. At last, the moment was perfect. And the surgery had gone perfectly.

It all started four years ago. There was no way around it – Maggie had to go for a hip replacement. As they held hands, tightly, in the doctor's rooms, their stomachs knotted. What would this mean? The pain? The risks? The recovery? The costs? And the waiting lists! The government health services were overwhelmed. This is something which could not wait. And yet they may be forced to. For months. And winter was coming, which would only make Maggie's suffering worse.

"But what about going abroad for surgery?" their doctor had asked. Dr Wilenkin, Boris, had been their family doctor forever. Heavens, he delivered Maggie and Brian's children, who now have their own children! Maggie and Brian knew Boris would never ask the question if he was not certain it was a safe, valid option.

What if? They wondered. And if so, where?

India. Boris was clear – India is where he would recommend. In his opinion, the medical care was amongst the best in the world, the nursing care was exceptional, and the facilities were the perfect blend of first-world standards with distinctly Asian warmth. And, most importantly, the waiting lists were short and the prices very competitive. Why not take a look?

Brian, being the academic of the family, started doing the research. And what he found was quite remarkable. India, a country once stereotyped as being rustic, had emerged as a powerhouse of technology and global competitiveness. And this extended from the IT sector to the medical sector. With some of the finest doctors, procedures, facilities and certifications in the world, and with government assertively promoting the Health Tourism sector, India was booming. Credibly and competitively. And after further investigation Brian found that they could get Maggie the medical care she needed in just four weeks' time. Not four months, but in just four weeks!

Excellent medical care, wonderful aftercare, elimination of long waiting lists, and even the airfare was reasonable. Why not?

And so they decided to go ahead. And now, just twelve weeks of recovery time later, here Brian stood, watching, smiling. He loves this woman. She was his heart. And seeing her move freely in anticipation of their guests arriving, he is grateful with all of his heart that Boris had brought India to them.

And with it, brought back Maggie's health... and her smile.

For any destination to operate as a solid, sustainable tourism economy the fundamentals of good business practice must be in place. Critical is consistency of supply and demand. In the case of the tourism sector this requires creating a destination proposition which offers year-round experiences, thereby creating year-round visitation.

Development of a 365 destination is essential to ensure that the tourism industry is able to create and sustain the key drivers of sector economic and societal growth. These include:

- employment,
- revenue generation,
- infrastructure development,
- trade,
- investor confidence,
- societal identity, and
- return on investment.

Engineering of a year-round destination, one which is relatively immune to changes in tourism flow due to climate and/or activity, demands careful definition of the tourism segments which make up the total destination proposition. Careful management of flows of travellers, those from both the leisure and business segments, is required across the year.

Because the reality is this:

A surge in tourism activity may create exciting, inspiring highs in economic activity, but unless the highs are sustained throughout the year, the lows will result in people working within the tourism industry being let go.

This results in a drop in household income, a dent in economic activity, decline in payment of utilities and school fees, and decrease in education of the next generation... until the next high season allows for re-employment, repayment, re-attendance and rebuilding.

The net effect: direct, dramatic weakening of the social fabric that keeps all of the people of the destination safe, warm and hopeful.

Central to this engineering of a year-round destination is the identification of *niche* tourism sectors which the destination can offer, and ideally *own*, as pillars of their total destination proposition.

Niche tourism – the formal development and investment into tourism sub-sectors which are carefully, creatively and clearly strategically designed and promoted to attract travellers with specific, often sophisticated special interests – are fundamental to the establishment of competitive, visionary destinations.

Eco-tourism, voluntourism, medical tourism, cultural tourism, cruise tourism, wine tourism, religious tourism – all of these are examples of niche sectors which destinations have leveraged as areas of destination proposition gravitas.

For example:

- INDIA, home of Ayurveda and now a world-class medical tourism sector.
- NEW ZEALAND, a centre of 100% pure eco-tourism.
- SOUTH AFRICA, where cultural tourism forms the backbone of the destination.
- SOUTH OF FRANCE, globally known as a centre of magnificent food & wine tourism.

- KENYA, a first thought when it comes to a classic, romantic African safari.
- DUBAI, with its exceptionally well established business tourism offering, immune to summer peaks in temperature.
- ALASKA, home of some of the world's finest boat and land-based whale and glacier watching.
- TAHITI, one of the world's leading honeymoon destinations.
- EGYPT's Red Sea, a mecca for the world's divers.

These sub-sectors become, in effect, tourism business units within the greater destination tourism offering. Their proposition is clear, their goals clearly defined, their target audiences and responding core messaging acutely carved out. Or, at least, they should be.

Often, niche tourism sub-sectors are created as secondary, temporary or tactical projects within the greater tourism sector mobilised for their incremental arrivals value alone. Such unfortunate occurrences suffocate the true potential of niche tourism. A great pity.

When developed and activated correctly, niche sub-sectors can in fact form the essential framework for destination competitiveness and traveller connectivity.

Visionary destinations, those building their tourism economy and tourism future through disciplined strategic management and commitment to legacy, recognise that the role of niche sectors is far more valuable than simply the numbers they bring.

Niche sectors not only have the ability to keep the fire burning, they can in fact determine the nature of the flame.

Their benefits are three-fold:

Firstly, and most obviously, niche tourism helps attract incremental arrivals. By resonating with specific target markets, niche tourism is able to attract visitation at, often, critical times of the year when the special interest is at its peak (ie. cyclical).

Cruising on the gracefully unfolding River Nile from Luxor to Aswan, for instance, has not only consistently increased Egypt's tourism numbers to the already popular destination through the invitation to visitors to travel for a period of one to two weeks in the comfort of a luxury, intimate cruise ship, it has also created a reason for visitors to return, offering traditional land-tour travellers a new perspective from which to view the ancient world. Memories of camel spotting along the banks of the river under a blissful blue sky become as penetrating as the first sight of the Sphinx in Giza.

Secondly, niche tourism allows for effective management of seasonality. By creating and activating niche sectors, which can attract visitation during low season periods, the industry is able to raise the baseline of sector employment and economic activity, sustaining tourism-related economic stability and prosperity, as well as social harmony and unity.

Dubai is a powerful example of utilising niche tourism to lift the seasonality curve. Known globally as a shopping mecca, Dubai not only actively promotes its exceptional ranges and rates to shoppers, it also activates major shopping events at key times of the year. One such event, the Summer Shopping Festival held annually in the peak of summer season in the sweltering desert destination, attracts over seven million shoppers to the emirate. Travellers from across the region and world flock to Dubai to enjoy exceptional bargain hunting, entertainment and eateries. The air-conditioning is turned up, the prices are brought down and the family fun is there for all to enjoy for a full month.

Lastly, and of exceptional strategic importance, niche tourism allows a destination to achieve essential shifts in destination perception. This is particularly important for destinations seeking to banish out-dated and/or incorrect perceptions of travellers (and the world at large) regarding national identity, quality and capability.

A wonderful example of this is India. Recognising the critical role which the tourism sector can play in building the nation for the future from the perspectives of employment, infrastructure, investment and poverty alleviation, the government made a conscious, clear, concrete commitment to sector development. The destination brand – simply incredible.

However, *'Incredible India'* still faced significant challenges with perceptions of cleanliness and sophistication of the destination. Already possessing a rich history in natural wellness and healing (*Ayurvedic* medicine) and with clear expertise amongst modern Indian medical doctors and services (with their affordability *vis a vis* western facilities), the government of India wisely identified Medical Tourism as a priority niche sector. This prioritisation was not only a means of attracting more visitors and building destination brand equity–it was a powerful way of getting the message out to the world that India is clean, safe, skilled and sophisticated. An incredible move for both tourism and healthcare advancement.

As shared by Sujit Banerjee, former Secretary, Ministry of Tourism, Government of India, and current Secretary-General, WTTC India Initiative:

> *"The Ministry of Tourism, Government of India, adopted Medical Tourism as a unique niche tourism product when it realised that not only are the costs involved ranging between one-third and one-tenth, but also that India can boast some of the best doctors and some of the best equipped JCI-compliant hospitals in the world.*
>
> *To create a medical tourism offering the product had to be wrapped up with the best pre- and post-operative care plus a bonus thrown in like a short stay in an Ayurveda Centre post-operation. Product development and international promotion became our focus. As a result Medical Tourism in India took a quantum jump, much beyond our expectations."*

To effectively, resource-efficiently and sustainably contribute to destination growth and development, the creation of niche sectors must play a part in the overall tourism growth strategy of the nation.

Specifically, niche sector development must clearly contribute to development of the sector through direct contribution to one of several of the following drivers of tourism economy growth:

- Increase in arrivals.
- Increase in yield.
- Increase in year-round visitation.
- Increase in dispersion of travellers outside of the main tourism hubs.
- Increase in destination brand equity.

- Increase in destination competitiveness.
- Increase in opportunity creation for people of the destination.

Therefore, before a destination identifies and seeks to develop a niche, some hard questions need to be asked including:
How does this niche support:

- the destination brand?
- momentum of arrivals?
- attracting new/repeat travellers?
- the overall image of the nation/region?
- lifting the seasonality curve in the low season?
- primary and secondary stakeholders?
- the greater tourism and economic development mandate?

What is the competitive landscape for the niche, and can we effectively, sustainably and credibly compete?

Is this a niche we can own?

Are we prepared to invest in the development and ongoing success of the niche to the point of:

- including it in the destination tourism strategy?
- providing adequate, ongoing resources – funds, people, and intelligence?
- creating policy to ensure sector support at all levels?

Why are we really wanting to do this?

- Who or what is the core motivation?
- What legacy will it leave for tourism, for other sectors and for the people of the destination?
- And how insulated is commitment to niche sector development from political change?

Answering, thoughtfully, the above questions will ensure that niche sector development acts as a fuel that allows the destination's future to burn brightly... protecting it from creation of a niche which may in fact burn quickly and powerfully but leave behind a destination damaged by its flames.

CHAPTER 12

DESTINATION DEVELOPMENT THROUGH MEDIA

They were so close...

For weeks, months in fact, Tim and Catherine had been planning their holiday. End of a tiring year, end of their energy, time to switch off...time to dive off. And they could not wait! The chance to leave behind the pressures of the big city. Chicago in exchange for two weeks on a dive boat in the middle of the Andaman Sea. All dives planned, all logistics taken care of, all luxuries included. Divine! The only thing they had to worry about was finding words to describe the colours of all of the creatures of the sea. And of course keeping an eye out for something large and hungry which may fancy a bit of foreign food!

But, last minute, because of Tim's work schedule, they had to change their plans. With immense disappointment travel schedules were adjusted, cancellations made. The desire to dive into a holiday in Asia turned into a quest to simply get away. Anywhere. Especially at the late stage of end of December when bookings were limited by availability and credit card capability. Both of them were deeply upset, but putting it into perspective they knew it was okay. The intention was to spend time together, wherever.

And so Christmas Day came and went on terra firma. By the time morning came on the 26th of December the diving holiday was a distant wish. New memories were being made.

Then the news broke. Across the Andaman Sea the waves were breaking at heights of 15 metres, crashing down upon shorelines, hotels, holiday makers. Holiday makers and locals woke (or were dramatically woken) the morning after Christmas to find the sea savagely pulling the shoreline into its flooding abyss. Resorts were ravaged, villages visciously torn apart. And unsuspecting families and communities also torn apart.

Offshore, the sea was swallowing up dive boats. The exact dive boats they had been booked on when there were still plans in place for a dive holiday. They were so close.

The international news readers called it a 'tsunami'. A new word was at that moment added to the global vocabulary.

All around, devastation. And the horror of natural disaster. Lives lost, hopes shattered. A future of recovery of not just the broken land, but the broken spirit of the people of the land.

They were so close.

Two years on, whenever they would think of a holiday, their thoughts seemed to keep drifting back to that time. That place.

But was the island ready for tourists again? It had only been two years. When the tsunami hit, it looked as though it would take the island a lifetime to recover. As much as they wanted to finally make the trip, was it the right time?

Following enquiries Tim was surprised to find that it was just a few weeks after the devastating incident occurred that the tourism authorities were actually sending out a very clear message to the world: If the tourism industry was to rebuild again tourists must come back. They must return to that beautiful corner of the Earth, stay longer, tip more. That is how the rebuilding, and healing, will occur.

And so, to close the loop, to feel some sense of closure on that haunting time, their almost-them moment, Tim and Catherine booked their tickets, booked their diving, and took the journey. They wanted, they needed to go back, to see the place they were almost a part of that fateful day. But this time to be tourists, helping rebuild the island's tourism industry for its people – a first step in rebuilding the lives of the locals.

Standing on the shoreline looking across the holiday resort beachfront, the damage was still visible, but even more apparent was the recovery of the industry, and the people who have taken back their destination from the sea. Buzzing, busy with tourists and smiling tourism industry employees, from the dive shop managers to the restaurant hosts to the fresh fruit stall sellers. Clearly it was the tourism industry, with the support of government and media letting the world know the destination is 'open for business', that has been the lifeboat, bringing back not just tourism dollars and investment, but the confidence and faith and pride of the people. The destination, and its people, will endure!

Months later, holding in her hands a string of pearls bought from a local artisan on a white-sand and tsunami warning-signed beachfront, it was impossible for Catherine not to attach a thought, a memory, an image, a story, to each and every pearl. As the pearls had been carefully strung together to hold tightly the beauty which they represent, so too had the people of the Andaman Sea resort town.

These are now Catherine's Tsunami pearls – her precious keepsake from a place which had rebuilt through tourism. And through her and Tim, in a small way, as travellers.

Media has become one of the most pervasive, permanent aspects of our lives. We expect it. We need it. We demand it. We are lost without it.

Importantly, media plays a critical role in how we make sense of our world from various perspectives, be they politically, socially, geographically, economically, spiritually, ideologically, culturally or environmentally.

As much as media can establish and build our perspective, it can also play a powerful role in *shifting* our perceptions. Media exposes us to, and updates us with, information and insight which can have a profound effect on our willingness to accept – or reject – something, someone or somewhere.

Nowhere is this truer than in the area of destination growth and development.

When it comes to travel & tourism, media has a powerful influence on the destination's brand and wider industry building efforts. Through the exceptional reach and richness of execution offered by media, destinations have the ability to share with the world 24/7/365 why they are different, why they are special, why they will fulfil traveller needs and why the time to visit is now!

For destinations this opportunity to enhance traveller knowledge, awareness, interest, urgency and connectedness to a place – touching them at meaningful emotional and engaging levels – can be the difference between arrivals and absences.

Media acts as a powerful tool for increasing competitiveness, sustainably and equitably.

Media choices and media voices have grown exponentially in recent times, now offering immediacy and individuality never before possible.

Once upon a time the media landscape was made up of a few familiar communications platforms. Traditional media (ie. television, radio, print, cinema and outdoor) provided a very acceptable array of destination marketing options which, when supported by direct marketing and CRM, made for a comfortable messaging outreach to target audiences.

And then the 21st century happened. Technology began (and continues to dramatically increase the media's ability to find target audiences anytime, anywhere. New media offerings are reaching people's phones, tablets and other personal devices. If a message can find you, it will. Few environments are sacred.

From a traditional media perspective, television is clearly the trusted foundation of destination brand and tourism business building. The importance of this vehicle for creating big brand reach and impact is proven. Television, with exceptional ability to reach worldwide audiences through high quality, high influence and trusted formats, is the essential bread and butter for destination brand building. Serious brands take television seriously. The television environment is not only a messaging platform, it is also a statement of the brand's credibility as a global player in the tourism market.

Outdoor offers an interesting option for destinations, especially when creatively brought to life in transport environments such as airports, subways, taxis and other public transport touchpoints.

Print, be it magazine or newspaper, can also have a place in the media mix, depending on the destination and the desired messaging impact.

On-line is a further, powerful magnification of big brand creation and continuity, allowing for click-through action from travel message to traveller conversion. With the ability to control content, carefully target audiences and quantify reach and response, on-line offers an important platform for destinations, on its own or as a follow-through to television.

And now there is social media, a game changer in communications, that has dramatically altered how the world is able to both receive and spread information and opinion. It is truly remarkable and empowering that one is now able to share ideas, information and opinions across borders, across cultures and across ideologies across the world.

All it takes is the click of a 'SEND' button and a thought can become thought leadership.

The role of social media in destination development has grown widely and loudly in curiosity, interest and budget commitment. YouTube, Twitter, Facebook and other communications communities are attracting more and more interest for audiences and advertisers. And more and more strength in ability to influence actions, reshape opinions and redefine performance.

These and other forms of social media have made it possible for tourism entities – airlines, airports, hotels, attractions, cities, etc. – to create affinity with millions of travellers, both planned and prospective. Sharing of latest information, announcements, offerings, advertising and events is now possible in low cost, low tech, high reach ways, connecting with travellers in their space, on their time. Unquestionably a powerful messaging vehicle.

There is, however, one catch. The communication flow of social media is two-way. Not only are advertisers able to message to the wide world of travel, travellers are able to express thought and opinion back. While advertisers normally apply caution and strategy to messaging, individuals (be they hotel guests, passengers, visitors to a destination) communicate more spontaneously, unedited and openly. The temptation to 'tell us what you think' and know that the world is reading can be too great to pass up, and may be too emotionally charged in the moment to consider the consequences of putting the message out there, forever. Right here, right now, it is about fifteen keystrokes of fame.

When this happens the impact of one opinion, magnified by the hundreds of millions (depending on the follower/friends/community size) can be massive. And not always positive. In one simple tweet a harsh critique of one passenger can create a wave of harsh commentary about an airline. A low rating of a restaurant caused by a bad service experience can prompt elimination of the eatery as an option for future patrons. A video clip of one single hotel room within a global hotel chain can result in cancellations of bookings.

But does social media have a role to play for tourism advertisers?

Absolutely. Social media deserves consideration as a tourism communications vehicle within the greater media mix *as long as* the destination has clearly defined specific communications objectives best met by the media type, carefully considered the impact that the social media vehicle may have on brand equity long term (ie. noting rub-off of brand media environment on greater brand image), and the motivation for usage of social media is 100% clear (ie. the right thing to do for the brand and bottom line, not just because others are saying it's the cool thing to do).

So many choices.

But how does one choose? What is the right media, right now?

As media options and opinions increase, the lines between strategy and tactics have become blurred for many destination advertisers. Fashionable media environments have started to push aside the familiar, often at the expense of the end-goal.

So how does the destination decide on what media to use, when, and with whom?

Once again it comes back to good business practices: having a clear destination vision and strategy, understanding the market and competitor landscapes, staying tuned with the ways in which travellers are evolving, and activating a media strategy which truly serves the communications goals and target audiences of the destination. The need for a thoughtful media strategy applies to destinations, airlines and airports as much as it does to hotels, resorts, events and attractions.

Ultimately, leaders of tourism destinations and businesses need to carefully examine a number of aspects when determining the media mix. These include:

- WHY is communication being considered? What is the objective of the messaging? Is it strategic Brand building? Or is the message more tactical in nature and desired effect?
- WHO is (are) the target audience(s) in terms of demographics, psychographics and travel motivations?
- WHERE should communication be trying to connect with these people in their life worlds? What touch points are being focused on, and how are these being maximised for effect and desired response?
- WHEN is the right time to be communicating with target audiences, ie. time of day, time of year? As well as before, during and after their travel experience?

- WHAT media should be used? What not? Why? And what does each media type say about the brand as a messaging platform?
- HOW are all media vehicles being integrated? How is media effectiveness being measured?

The above questions will help shape a strategically grounded communications strategy for the destination, maximising message, messenger and monies invested.

But it does not end there.

In addition to a destination developing a solid tourism communications strategy, it is vital that it develops solid, pro-active relationships with leading media. Finding, connecting with, educating and investing in a media partner should only be done with media who, through their business philosophy, practices and track record, demonstrate a sense of vision, strategic know-how and responsibility to turn tourism advertising of destinations, hotels, resorts, airlines, airports, attractions, events – whatever the case may be.

Effective media exposure is not about *quantity* of presence, it is about *quality* – quality of message, quality of messenger (ie. media network) and quality of audience (target travellers and opinion leaders).

Similarly, it is not about best rates and rebates. It is about best reach, creative solutions and commitment to long-term growth. By bringing to life the destination brand.

Support of the media as an advertising partner goes beyond simply for when the destination is managing the business of tourism. Fortunately, there are global media leaders who fundamentally understand the role of media in nation building, and are prepared to work with destinations responsibly, strategically and creatively to build their tourism economies.

As stated by Rani Raad, Senior Vice-President & Managing Director CNN International Ad Sales and Business Development:

"The media is playing a critical role in stimulating sustainable tourism growth. The past decade has seen a dramatic increase in the number and type of media platforms being offered to advertisers seeking to build destination brand awareness and appeal. This growth in messaging environments has created new opportunities, but also new risks, as far as the brand's ability to reach audiences.

For this reason advertisers need to work with their media partners to ensure that destinations are utilising the correct media platform and messages to reach target audiences in a timely, impactful and cost-effective manner. CNN *continues to be at the forefront of the development and application of media to meet the strategic and tactical needs of our clients in the tourism industry, across the globe. We have a reputation for innovation, and are proud to set new standards in our strategic client services."*

This commitment of leading media entities to governments and businesses operating within the tourism sector, has been a critical part of tourism industry success, especially over the past decade.

Especially when things go wrong.

What is often overlooked is the important role which the media plays when a crisis occurs and a destination's tourism sector is brought to a standstill. When faced with disaster, be it acts of God or acts of man, travellers make assumptions about the state of the tourism industry – its ability to offer travellers a local experience both in terms of infrastructure and spirit. Safety and security, as well as experience satisfaction, become doubted. When things go horribly wrong the natural assumption is that it will take some time before things are right again.

The ability for a destination to recover and rebuild its infrastructure *and its image* becomes heavily dependent on the destination's ability to communicate to the world that it is *'open for business'*.

Over the past decade an array of disasters – natural and manmade – have hit the world and its tourism sector. From SARS to the tsunami, 9/11 and H1N1, destinations across the globe have had their tourism industry thrown into periods of paralysis. Destinations have had to fight through these challenges to re-mobilise the industry and encourage travellers to return. Similarly a number of nations have emerged into a new liberation. The end of wars, the redefinition of borders, the beginning of new political eras, and the advancement of societies have all played a part in shifting nations from states of destruction to states of peaceful security.

As destinations have (re)emerged and evolved as new geographies, new societies, new economies and centres of new opportunity the ability for the world to understand and embrace their new ethos has had much to do with the way in which the nation has expressed itself to internal and external audiences *from a communications perspective.*

During times of crisis when the destination is in the headlines, in-the-moment communication conveys the story of the situation. Once the crisis has concluded, the communications silence coming from the destination creates assumptions in the minds of travellers around the state of the destination in terms of ability to reopen the tourism industry.

These assumptions more often than not are far worse than the reality, causing dangerous delays to destination recovery. Consequently the destination is stunted in its ability to get back on its feet again, operationally and emotionally, as there are no tourists to welcome, to go back to work for, to become excited about.

Destination advertising is vital to destination building and destination recovery. Not only does it put out the welcome mat for travellers, it reignites the spirit and sense of determination of the people of the destination to unite as proud, productive, ready hosts.

For destinations and tourism businesses to thrive, partnership with the media is critical. The right media. Those that deserve the honour of working alongside destinations shaping their future, one visitor and one viewer at a time.

CHAPTER 13

FESTIVALS – TOURISM CALLING BY CANDLELIGHT

"When are we going to Japan together? We seem to keep putting it off whenever we plan our holidays. Why not this Christmas?"

She had to admit it, it was terribly amusing listening to him get all excited about planning their year-end break, in September!

For all the time she has known him she has always known him to be booking his flights on the way to the airport! Last minute was in his DNA – he loved the game of waiting until all of the websites and search engines were checked, prices compared and best options discovered. Sometimes it seemed to her that the hunt for the fare was part of the holiday fun.

Indeed, opposites attract! She preferred counting sleeps – booking well in advance so that she could savour the lead-up anticipation and avoid the last minute adrenaline. As long as they ended up in the same place, at the same time, she was fine with his way of doing things.

But in this case timing was not up to the websites or the search engines if they were wanting to go to Japan and capture the moments which they had in their hopes and hearts for their first time in that lovely part of Asia. It was up to Mother Nature.

And she was clear: it has to be spring. Because that is when the cherry blossoms are all out in their magnificent glory, and when the Cherry Blossom Festivals take place. Just the thought of it made her smile – magnificent Japanese architecture standing with generations-old charm and enchantment, surrounded by an orchard of cherry trees all transformed into fluffy, fragrant clouds of pink from the millions of blossoms opening to welcome Spring. There standing alongside she imagined beautiful Japanese women, dressed in their finest silks to celebrate the season, with sweet children running through the trees with their fragrant blossoms, catching petals like snowflakes falling from the sky.

For years she had dreamt of travelling to Japan, seeing the country through that soft white and pink haze. The haze of the cherry blossoms...

That was the time to go. When the trees were in bloom.

So, where should they call in the new year, she wondered? Which country is known for its holiday celebrations at that time of year? Hmmm, she thought... what about Rio?

Véspera de Ano Novo.

Suddenly the image of the festival of calling in the new year, with its millions of people, all dressed in white, releasing thousands of floating candles into the sea off Copacabana beach, filled her mind and heart.

Perfect!

Throughout the year, across the globe, people of diversely different countries and cultures share one common habit – they mark special days on their calendars when candles and evening skies light up with festival lights!

From Eid to Divali, Christmas to Carnival, Hanukkah to Hanami, Stampedes to Sopot, Mardi Gras to Maslenitsa, and so many more special occasions, festivals act as fabulous magnets for the spirits of millions. Across generations, time zones and technical locations a world of people come together to celebrate.

Literally thousands of festivals take place across the world each year. Annual celebrations of nations, regions and communities inspire a pause for people to pay respect to their beliefs. Be it to celebrate the seasons of life (literally and/or figuratively), or the traditions and religions of both ancient and modern time, festivals bring people together to share who they are, what they believe in, what they love, what they are grateful for, what makes them a proudly united community.

What better time to invite the world to enjoy a destination than festival time?

With today's travel & tourism industry so fiercely competitive, destinations – those well established and those well on their way as emerging stars – are fighting for airtime, artistic stand-out, awareness, appreciation and booking action. Promises of experiences, emotion and endless possibility for pleasure abound. Some destinations sparkle, some are magical, some are breathtaking, some are simply incredible.

Through all of the competition and campaigning, there is one edge that every destination across the world has at its disposal – a competitive advantage so often overlooked: its festivals.

Extending a unique form of invitation to the world's travellers, festivals bring to life the energy, engagement and emotion of a destination like few other experiences.

Take Divali for example. Once a year India, and Indians around the world, celebrate the festival of light (both Hindus and non-Hindus, interestingly). Inspired by the story of Rama and Sita from the epic 27,000 verse Sanskrit poem *The Ramayan* Divali is a time of celebration of good over evil, of light over darkness, of virtue and purity and faith. From cities to villages, homes to hotels, Divali is a spirit which connects India from north to south, west to east.

In true Indian style the occasion takes place over several days. As Divali nears days and nights become filled and focused on decorating and gifting, friends, family and feasting. Floors become canvases for paints and petals creating brightly coloured shapes reflective of the season. Oranges and pinks and whites and yellows burst onto sidewalks and entranceways, accented with tiny candles and diyas (oil lamps) burning a gold light to add a magical glow to the colourful sight. And finally, when Divali actually arrives and prayers are said, the night sky lights up with an array of sparkling, popping, colour-splashing fireworks much to the delight of children running about with their sparkler sticks. Infectious music, oh-so-delicious food, divine sweets, generous amounts of embraces and laughter, and a pageant of magnificent fashions and jewels from across India's radiant style spectrum send a clear message – this is *incredible India!*

The same applies to thousands of other festivals around the world inspired by religion, tradition, nature and history. Each and every occasion holds within its celebrations a rich, unique expression of the destination's people, culture and spirit – bringing the concept of experiential travel to life in ways which are deeply touching, deeply memorable and deeply inspiring.

Festivals are powerful marketing opportunities. Incorporating festivals into marketing strategies is not, however, simply the addition of a vehicle to the marketing mix. The value of festivals to destination building – brand and metrics – is far more strategic than that.

Importantly, festivals offer a destination the opportunity to achieve a number of strategic imperatives central to sector growth and development – imperatives which, technically speaking, exist within every tourism and economic development mandate across the world.

These include:

- **Increasing yield:** Travellers bring undeniable value to a destination. Quantitatively when the tourism community 'counts' the value of travellers we often default to the metric of number of arrivals. Growth in numbers of tourism arrivals does not mean growth in tourism receipts (revenues). As an example, a destination which cut prices on links in the experience chain may successfully increase arrivals but may in fact weaken total tourism receipts.

  The goal is to increase the value of receipts of each and every traveller – the amount of money which each traveller injects into the economy through various aspects of their visit, be it accommodation, meals, transport, attractions, purchasing of gifts in the destination, etc.

  Number of Arrivals x Receipts per Traveller = Yield.

  Festivals have the ability to increase the *Yield* of travellers, increasing not only the quantity (Arrivals) of visitors to the destination but also the quality (Receipts) of visitors.

- **Increasing length of stay:** Festivals create time-framed, culture-intense, stimulus-soaked experiences for travellers to plan for, schedule around and partake in. Often a motivation in their own right, or as an extension to a planned journey to a destination, festivals can become a fabulous bow on top of a travel experience. As a result, festivals have the ability to increase the length of a traveller's stay, and therefore increase yield. And, of course, festivals, like mega events, create a good reason to '*go now*', creating a sense of urgency to undertaking a planned holiday.

- **Year-round visitation:** In peak holiday periods people of the destination directly and indirectly employed by the tourism economy are busy busy busy transporting visitors, serving meals, selling goods, making beds, performing, touring – doing all the things which a destination needs to offer meaningful traveller experiences. As the high season slides down into the low season, there are significantly less visitors to host. Employment within the industry drops off, creating disturbing troughs in economic and social activity.

  One of the most valuable aspects of festivals, strategically placed, is that they have the ability to spread travellers throughout the year. Traditional low seasons can be meaningfully and sustainably boosted by showcasing a festival to attract inflows of tourism activity and therefore keeping the tourism economy switched on and in a healthy operating hum, flattening seasonality curves.

- **Increasing distribution of travellers:** Similarly, festivals are a powerful way of spreading travellers across the destination, moving them out of the gateway cities and into further places and pockets of interest. As a result activity and benefits of the tourism industry and economy can be shared across the destination as opposed to held in traditional, often iconic traveller nodes. Opportunity is created to showcase lesser known aspects of the destination – different peoples, different cultures, different traditions, different histories and different environments.

And of course:

- **Repeat visitation:** What better reason to return to a much-loved destination than to experience a much celebrated festival?

  In the same way that tourism products and experiences are put under the spotlight as shining examples of what the destination has to offer culturally, historically, in art, tradition and future focus, festivals act as beautifully packaged soundbytes of the spirit, energy, creativity and aspects of pride of a destination.

  The ability to attract significant visitation, especially in off-season times of the tourism year, reinforces the need for destination development and marketing strategies to take into consideration festivals as powerful, meaningful destination-building sparks.

Festivals, with all their energy, excitement and anticipation, add inspiring and highly enticing news value to destination campaigns. And of course, and of great importance, intensify the sense of pride and spirit of welcoming amongst the people of the destination.

CHAPTER 14

MAJOR EVENTS – MAJOR DRIVERS OF TOURISM GROWTH

Staring at the field, surrounded by 90,000 spectators, Tsepho could feel his heart pounding in his chest. Despite the chill of South African winter winds blowing, he felt nothing but glow – a warm inner glow. And childlike excitement!

In just over one hour the first whistle will blow on the 2010 FIFA WORLD CUP in South Africa. Finally, following 12 years of visioning, 6 years of organisation, an estimated US$ 4 billion in direct capital investment, selection of 32 international teams, and millions of man-hours of preparations, KE NAKO – it's time!

Tsepho, along with 49 million fellow South Africans, was watching with the world watching alongside. A life-long dream was about to come true.

For each and every South African the hosting of the 2010 FIFA World Cup was a remarkable project in national investment. Packaged as an international mega event, the 2010 Games were the greatest single injection of investment the nation had seen since its liberation in 1994.

A national upgrade programme, the 2010 Games demanded that the country got to work, ensuring that the fundamentals were well in place to host the largest, most watched sporting event on earth.

In addition to World Cup infrastructure projects, Tsepho had heard that money was also channelled towards non-infrastructure projects – sports and recreation programmes, arts and culture programmes, policing, emergency medical services and telecommunications upgrades. Immense amounts of investment spent on, effectively, a sporting event, in a nation hungry for the foundations required by a society busy rebuilding itself.

So naturally Tsepho wondered: Why would his country make such an investment into what could be simply a tourism event? Why not hospitals and schools and utilities? Why this, now?

The leaders of his country had been tirelessly spreading the message from the very beginning – it was because of what would be built beyond 2010, once the Games had ended, the champions been crowned, the fans departed and the stadium lights turned off. Tsepho's country would never, ever be the same.

Even before the Games had begun he could feel the change. It started long ago, on May 15th, 2004 when South Africa had been awarded 2010 World Cup host nation status. That was a day that unlocked the nation's future. There was no looking back...

And now, looking out over the magnificent stadium with thousands and thousands of fans from all over the world, waving their flags and blowing their vuvuzelas (or at least trying to!), almost hypnotised by the overwhelming soccer fanatical hum swallowing him up Tspeho's thoughts started to drift.

"What if we hadn't?" he thought to himself. "What would the streets look like? What would our roads and bus systems and police look like? How would these people from across the world look at us? How would we look at ourselves?"

They are not defining moments, they are RE-defining moments.

But what if South Africa hadn't hosted the 2010 Games? It was hard for Tsepho to even imagine. Thankfully he didn't have to.

Because right here, right now, he and every single South African across the country and world were celebrating, as one nation, swelling with pride and new possibility.

They had done it! The Games were beginning, the future was beginning.

Indeed, it's time!

The Olympic Games. The FIFA World Cup. The Commonwealth Games. The Paralympic Games. The Cricket World Cup. The Rugby World Cup.

For athletes of the world these (and many other) major sporting events represent the highest point of achievement on the international sporting stage. With the eyes of the world watching, athletes are given the opportunity to prove that they are among, and possibly are, the best in the world. Prominence, pre-eminence, profile and power – these are outcomes of being seen to play a part in the Games.

Yet to earn the right to play a part takes years of preparation. Significant investment of time, energy and money are prerequisites. One has to really want to be able to win a place on the podium. And one must make every second of the Games worth it, maximising the benefit of being able to say *"I was there"*. Because those few days of competition can change a life forever.

Winning a place in the Games is not the only competition involved in major sporting events. Equally fierce is the competition to win the right to be the place *where* the Games are held.

Like aspiring athletes, aspiring host cities seek their moment of fame, the opportunity to show the world what they can do better than anyone, and anywhere, else. To be awarded the title and immense honour of 'host city' of a major international sporting event can have as profound an effect on a city, region and nation as on an athlete. It can change the profile of the place, and lives of the people, forever.

To take on the responsibility of host city (or nation) of a major sporting event demands unprecedented levels of commitment to delivery of a very tightly defined, carefully watched and painstakingly engineered set of contracted deliverables that will be defined by the Games' 'owners' – the IOC, FIFA, ICC, IRB, etc. For an extended period of time the event grabs hold of the best of the city's/nation's resources – people, time, funds – taking over personal lives and professional careers. There is zero margin for executional error, zero opportunity for Plan Bs, zero space to exhale. And this is even before the Games begin.

So why do destinations do it? Why is being host city or nation so important? Why turn a place seemingly upside down for a few days of sport? A few locations of play? A few special athletes?

It's all about one little word with massive impact: Legacy.

The chance to play host to a major event is an exceptional opportunity to shape the future of the nation, especially its tourism sector. And with that, to magnify the multiplier effect of the tourism economy, and the greater spirit of the people of the nation itself.

As a powerful example of the power of major events: the 2010 FIFA World Cup in South Africa. South Africa's hosting of the FIFA World Cup in June 2010 represented so much more than 30 days of football. Even for this football-loving nation.

Timing of hosting was critical.

Back in May 2004 when South Africa bid for the title of host nation of the 2010 FIFA World Cup, leaders of the national bid team knew very well the impact that winning would have on national image advancement – within and outside South Africa. The moment Sepp Blatter, President of FIFA, opened the envelope and revealed South Africa's success in its bid, not only did the joy at the moment of announcement allow President Nelson Mandela to feel like a 16 year old teenage boy again while tearfully holding the World Cup tight, the moment also set South Africa on a six year path of national reconstruction – physically and emotionally.

Interestingly preparations for the Games since 2004 have insulated the nation from the worst of the impact of the 2008/9 global economic downturn. Whilst the building sector globally came to a grinding halt due to the lack of availability of credit and the high cost of materials, as a result of pre-committed, pre-funded Games preparations thousands of workers involved in 2010 FWC infrastructure projects across the country remained employed. Progress had been maintained. And of critical importance, the people of the nation remained focused on the day the opening whistle of the Games will blow on June 11th, 2010. The spirit of the nation remained positive and inspired.

In the end the Games provided a unifying reason for investment into tourism infrastructure, and a commitment to delivery and clarity regarding the value beyond the event.

2010 was about 2011, 2012, 2013...

As expressed by Dr Laurine Platzky, Deputy Director-General, 2010 FIFA World Cup Co-ordinator in the Department of the Premier, in the Western Cape (home of host city Cape Town):

"Imagine if we had not had the World Cup. Would we by now have housed and employed all the people in the city? Would we, with all those billions spent on the World Cup, instead have educated all our children, fed the hungry and restructured our city – probably not because we would still have been arguing on how to do it all. Forgive me but without a tight deadline, budget and dedicated teams of skilled people, structural change is not possible. Nothing like time and money to focus the mind."

From the perspective of the tourism economy, with major events come the potential for dramatic increases in a number of critical destination growth and development metrics. These include:

- **Arrivals:** Athletes, support teams, media, officials and fans arriving into the destination from across the country and across the world for the Games, and for pre- and post-Games touring.
- **Revenues:** Money spent by visitors spending time in the destination over the period of the Games, as well as pre- and post-stays.
- **Investment:** Money injected into the destination for critical infrastructure development.
- **Employment:** The tens of thousands of people employed in the array of roles needed to make the event happen – *before, during* and *after* the Games.
- **Skills development:** Knowledge and skills transfer which result from Games preparations and activation and which remain in the minds and lives.
- **Environmental management:** Engineering environmentally-responsible methods of design and operation into new and/or upgraded infrastructure, *'greening the Games'*.
- **Identity:** Building of profile of the destination as a host city/nation through media exposure of the event.
- **Unity:** The natural effect of the coming together of the people of the host city/nation.

For this reason, major sporting events are actively sought after by governments. The long-term benefits should outweigh the short-term cost. Through major events critical initiatives can be addressed, core attitudes shifted, key strategic priorities fulfilled. For a limited period of time, national treasuries are willingly turned into giant ATMS (with withdrawal limitations, of course), channelling funds into major, mandatory infrastructure projects required for the events.

Putting aside all of the glitz, glamour, grand excitement and great blessing of hosting a major sporting event, Games execution must be understood and positioned by the destination as a strategic lever within the greater tourism growth and development strategy.

Form and fanfare must follow strategic function.

It is critical that major sporting events maximise short-term efforts for the long-term benefit of the destination to truly BUILD the destination:

- **B:** Directly reflecting, and overtly driving, the essence of the destination **brand**.
- **U:** Working to **unite** the people of the destination, and its visitors, closer together in pride, in interaction, and in upliftment of quality of life.
- **I:** Ensuring **infrastructure** supports delivery of both hard (transport systems, energy, stadiums, telecommunications, safety and security, accommodation, etc.) and soft (service culture, skills development, brand delivery, policy, marketing and promotion, partnerships, etc.) areas of the experience.
- **L:** Investing in the **legacy** of the tourism sector – creating today what will become the building blocks of tomorrow, clearly communicating the long-term benefits and responsibility of continued delivery of the event.
- **D:** Dramatically enhancing the destination's ability to **deliver** the tourism brand promise to travellers.

Through it all expectations must be carefully managed.

Of great importance, leaders must ensure that the stakeholder community is clear that:

- hosting a major event is not a short-term project. It is a destination-evolving programme.
- exceptional care must be taken to not exploit the opportunity of hosting by abusing pricing. Major events are not an early retirement plan.
- with great power of event leadership comes great responsibility. Transparency is vital.
- the real work of making the event work for the destination starts *after* the event is over.

The benefits of hosting a major sporting event can be as wide reaching, deeply penetrating and long lasting as the vision of the leadership of the local government and people of the destination.

While there may only be one gold, one championship trophy and one MVP, when it comes to hosting major sporting events, winning goes far beyond the athletes.

When the rules of hosting the Game are mastered, and the role of the tourism sector is played correctly, the host city/nation can only come out on top.

Let the Games begin!

CHAPTER 15

THE ROLE OF FILM IN DESTINATION DEVELOPMENT

Fortunately it was so early in the morning it did not take too much time to get a taxi. The sight of a London black cab always made Nandni smile. They looked like children's storybook images brought to life. And the taxi drivers made for such animated conversation. "London Paddington – Heathrow Express" the hotel doorman stated to the driver. And she was off.

Sitting in the back of the taxi she looked around at the colours which the streets of London took on at this time of year, this time of day. She loved this city. Even if visiting for business. She loved its charm and character. And how easy it was to connect to the rest of the world.

"So, where are you off to?" the taxi driver asked? "Anywhere nice?"

"Poland", she replied. "Business. But it is still beautiful. But no time to really look around."

For a moment she hesitated – did she really want to get chatty with the driver? This early? Actually, yes. This is London – she knew she would learn something from him, and probably something that would leave her smiling.

"So where do you go off to when you take a holiday?" she enquired.

"Greece. Just got back. One of the best trips ever." His response was full of energy, enough to make him slide open the little window between the front and back of the taxi. "We went to an island called Kefalonia. You remember the movie 'Captain Corelli's Mandolin'? They filmed it there, in Kefalonia. And they even left the old village they recreated."

Nandni knew the spot immediately. Or at least she remembered the scenes from the movie. And suddenly the stereotypical images in her mind's eye of thousands of tourists scattered around the usual 'destination Greece' islands. Ios and Santorini for example, were replaced with charming, soft, romantic and rustic images she remembers from the movie. Images which are now nine years old, considering the movie was produced in 2001.

As she boarded her plane for Poland, those images remained with her... a lovely reminder of a place of immense beauty, and a clear reminder of her need to plan her next holiday.

Between the period of October 5th and 8th, 2009, government leaders from within the travel & tourism world united in Astana, Kazakhstan for the 18th Annual General Assembly of the UNWTO. Over a thousand members of the tourism community, including Ministers of the over 155 member countries in 7 regions, along with over 400 Affiliate members – the 'A List' of tourism at government level – gathered for annual deliberations, as well as the confirmation of Mr Taleb Rifai as the new Secretary-General. United in a quest to increase the profile and understanding of the sector as a major force for social and economic development worldwide, in a year where the global economic crisis and H1N1 pandemic have taken a direct hit at the sector, leaders of global travel & tourism travelled to Astana committed to impact, unity and contribution.

Kazakhstan proved to be a wonderful host nation for the UNWTO's Annual General Assembly. A relatively new nation on the world map, Kazakhstan's streets reflect an energy of dramatic change, grand vision and modern ambition. Astana is a young city waiting for the world. Its exceptional city planning structure and unique architecture make it very clear – Kazakhstan is on the world stage as a strong, serious, shiny new player!

Unfortunately, prior to arriving in Kazakhstan most participants did not have a spontaneous mental image of the country or city to seed anticipation of arrival. More often than not, however, mention of imminent travel to Kazakhstan prompted an immediate, inescapable response from family, friends and associates prior to the trip: *"Borat!"*

Even today it is the movie and its infamous lead character who defines the identity of this nation. He and his antics have embedded in Kazakhstan a tainted sense of the place and its people – who they are, what they look like, how they think, how they live their lives. While understood to be a movie and therefore dosed with a high degree of exaggeration for entertainment purposes, people around the world exposed to just the trailer of the movie, or the flurry of PR generated by the film, hold direct associations between the name of the nation and the very original, to some audiences very funny and most often very offensive character *Borat*. Such a shame.

Borat is an exceptional example of the power of film in building destination awareness. And the importance of managing the impact on destination identity.

Over the past decade the film industry has become a highly sought after vehicle for destination development. National and regional tourism authorities are investing more and more time, money and energy into courting film studios to come to their country and cities to shoot, opening up the landscapes, street systems and communities to film crews. High levels of information and incentives are put forward to persuade studios to set up camp.

Featuring a destination in a film can be through a number of formats including:

- The destination as a filming environment, as occurred in films such as *The Lord of the Rings*. The nation's magnificent natural, blank canvas enabled the creators of the film to bring a fictitious trilogy to life in a nation which only through film promotion was revealed to be New Zealand.
- A city/country-identifiable location for films seeking unique locations with the cachet of iconic imagery. *Angels and Demons*, for example, turned the Vatican City into a fabulous backdrop for a story which, much through its movie recreation, generated understanding and interest in the home of a global religion. Similarly, the highly successful Stieg Larsson *Millennium* Trilogy which turned the girl with the dragon tattoo into a worldwide book and movie phenomenon, has been enticing travellers to the chilly, seedier sides of Stockholm to trace the steps of the enigmatic lead character. And there is Bollywood, a destination in itself, that has started turning iconic international cities such as Cape Town into backdrops for its, increasingly, globally appreciated Indian films.
- Creating a character out of the location of the film, as was done with *Sex and The City, the Movie* (and the television series, of course) – a production which overtly defines NYC to be the '5th lady',
- and the grand prix, incorporating the destination as a part of the film's name and storyline, as occurred, for example, with the epic production of *Australia* – effectively a two and a half hour product placement for the destination and its magnificent Outback. Similarly, *Vicky Christina Barcelona* provided audiences with a wonderful expose of Spain's attraction-rich city on the Mediterranean coastline.

  There are a number of clear benefits which come from offering a destination for filming. In addition to exposure, there are the often unseen gains to the destination. These include:

  - **Income:** Money brought to the destination through the local purchase of materials, supplies, accommodation, internal travel, vehicle and prop hire, etc.

- **Investment:** Funds injected into the destination for building of sets and supporting infrastructure needed by the film, and which often remain in the destination after the film crews have left.
- **Employment:** Job creation for locals in the areas of set creation, support services, catering, and other production-related elements, as well as inclusion as extras.
- **Skills development:** Training given to locals to assist with the various aspects of production, skills which remain with local employees long after the film's creators have departed.
- **Media:** Feature of the destination in pre-publicity, features on the film including 'the making of' programmes.
- **Awareness:** The very real exposure which the destination receives which not only educates viewers around the destination and its scope of natural, cultural, social and emotional offerings, but entices travellers to visit to experience it all for themselves. Film can be an exceptional fuel for T&T sector growth, development and competitiveness.

All of the above are strong motivations and justifications for a destination rolling out the red carpet to the international film industry.

There are very real risks involved with destination appearances in films. These risks come as a result of the destination not recognising and/or owning the result of the destination awareness created by the film.

Awareness does not mean positive image.

Creation of a film in and/or about a destination requires conscious, pro-active, comprehensive destination image management on the part of the destination, especially its tourism sector. Giving credit where it is due, *Borat* was very valuable to Kazakhstan to put the nation in the mind-map of people of the world. But once people learnt of it and had an initial sense of the people, the spark needed to be fuelled from there by the nation's leaders of national image and identity. As a result of only a low level of reactive destination marketing, the image of *Borat* rubbed off quickly and deeply onto Kazakhstan. And is not unlike a tattoo on the nation's image.

India faced the risk of a similar situation with the unexpected, magical success of *Slumdog Millionaire*. There was significant concern that the image of the slums would create over-riding assumptions about the identity on India. This did not happen, however, as destination India has for the past 5+ years managed its national image and identity development incredibly. It was therefore possible to position the film's story, success and subsequent benefits to the nation within the greater national identity – a colour of the prism, not the material of the crystal.

Despite the temptation to make it onto the big screen (or even the little screen), tourism leaders need to hit the 'pause' button before giving the go-ahead to start shooting.

The concept of putting a destination into a film needs to be screen-tested, looked at carefully from every angle

and examining the following:

- How is the destination being used? Is it an identifiable character in the storyline, or simply an anonymous backdrop?
- What will the film's storyline say about the destination, if anything at all?
- What opportunities are there to promote the destination alongside the film?
- Will destination exposure through the film help attract tourists? And if so, what type of tourists?
- Will film production create opportunity for local investment? Skills development? Employment? Casting of extras?
- How can we support the film company when they are here as far as hosting, logistics and approvals are concerned?
- How can we attract future film business from this opportunity?
- Why are we really doing this? Is it the fun? The fame? Is it fundamentally the right thing to do?

There is no question that the film industry can be one of the greatest blessings for a destination to be able to establish traveller awareness, appeal, affinity and ultimately inspire travel booking action.

Therefore, like all tourism sector development initiatives,

the role of film needs to be an active part of the destination's growth and development strategy.

When it comes to destinations becoming stars in the film industry, the bottom line can be rich and enriching, as long as all aspects of impact are taken into account.

It's all about being red carpet ready.

CHAPTER 16

VOLUNTOURISM – MAKING A POSITIVE DIFFERENCE

He never thought it would happen to him. Sure, he knew the stats. The headlines repeatedly showcasing the rise of failed relationships and the fall of the institution of marriage. He knew it was always possible. But that happened to other people, not him! Until it did.

And now, stuck in the reality of it all, his inner light had gone out. And he knew it. Sadly so did others. As hard as he tried to fight back with a quick "I'm fine!" whenever anyone asked, no one believed him. They say he had lost his smile.

He needed to get away.

But not to sit on a beach. Not to do the clubs of a big bright city. Not to spend days touring magnificent castles and temples which he would be unable to appreciate – his eyes for beauty were simply shut. He needed to be alone. Be anonymous. Be someone else. And to think of a life other than his own.

He remembers precisely the moment he realised what it was he needed. He was watching the news. And as always, the headlines were filled with stories of war, loss, longing for a better life. There was just so much need out there. But where does one begin to help? How can one single person make an impact on the world when the world needs so much?

Also, as much as he wanted to help, he didn't want to just give money. He was not 100% sure that the funds would reach the people who needed them, 100% intact. But maybe he could help? Maybe he could be there, making a difference, by making his time and energy work for others as they are rebuilding their lives? Maybe this was it?

And so he began the search for a trip which would allow him to get away yet help others. What he never expected to find was that not only were these types of 'holidays' possible, they had an official name – Voluntourism. Digging deeper into the options, he found himself gravitating towards the Andes. With little effort yet much excitement he found it – this is where he wanted to be and what he wanted to be doing. Building a school and teaching English in a small village in the Andes. Four weeks, fourteen flying hours away from home in Geneva, four hours trekking up into the mountains from the nearest town, forty village families, four hours a day building, four hours a day teaching children and adults.

That was six months ago. And yet it is as fresh as yesterday.

And yet that other man, the broken man he left behind at the airport when embarking on this journey, feels like a lifetime ago. Because today, because of the time spent taking care of others, helping others, teaching others, and building for others, he carries with him what once was lost and now is found...

In the Andes he found his smile.

Without a doubt the dawning of the twenty first century has brought with it a sense of the world waking up. Major events, both of natural and man-made consequence, from 9/11, the tsunami of 2006, the earthquake in Haiti in the first days of 2010, and other global events, have caused people around the world to look around and question not just how it all fits together, but how they fit in. Events on one side of the globe are now felt on another. Growth in global communication is causing a growth in global awareness and compassion. A sense of *"it has to be about more than just me"* is emerging.

Generation 'I' of the past is making way for Generation 'Why' of the present.

This heightened sense of collective conscience is having an impact on the way travellers view the world. Being there, seeing that and buying the T-shirt is no longer enough. Increasingly travellers are seeking experiences which allow them to get closer to the places they visit.

Making an impact, making a difference, has become an important part of making a holiday meaningful.

As a result the quest to discover new places and people, becoming a participant in their world and not simply a passer-by, has given life to a powerful new tourism niche: Voluntourism.

Voluntourism, also referred to as Edu-Tourism and Volunteer Travel, effectively turns holiday time into a project. The fusion of getting away and giving back caused a dramatic rate of growth over the past ten years. More and more travellers are wanting to combine down-time with social responsibility. This niche, while small at present, is proving to be an invaluable fuel for the (re)building of local communities in need of support, be they skills, muscle power or otherwise.

While the size of the voluntourism niche sector is up for debate, interest in voluntourism is not. All research shows arrows up. Study after study on the segment reveals a growing interest in turning one or more of their annual get-aways into a time to give back.

The nature of the projects varies as widely as the nations in which they are conducted. Voluntourism spans across a number of areas of activity. In some destinations the need is language skills, e.g. teaching English in villages in rural India. In others it is conservation, e.g. rhino protection in South Africa. In others it may be restoration, e.g. preservation of the Terracotta Warriors in China. And in others it may in fact be post-crisis recovery of communities, e.g. following devastation to coastal villages in Thailand and Sri Lanka following the tsunami. The need is great, the choices vast, the experiences enriching. And, importantly, the conditions of participation are few. Travellers from six to sixty six can take part in voluntourism projects.

The scope of projects offered across the globe makes it possible for travellers across the age, skills, fitness and comfort spectrum to find a project which taps into their desires.

A 2009 study conducted by GeckoGo[7] found that, of the over 2,400 respondents from across Asia, Europe and North America (most between 25 and 34 years of age), multiple interests existed, with:

- 62% wanting to do humanitarian work;
- 56% interested in conservation and teaching;
- 53% interested in community development;
- 28% looking to work on construction projects.

Importantly, voluntourists do not seek payment for their contribution – what is gained from the experience can be simply priceless. The quest to do good far exceeds the desire to make good money.

Nations creating voluntourism as a key niche for tourism sector development create an ability for travellers to play a part in destination sustainability. The ethos of the destination is shared, practically, with visitors. And the destination brand takes on a strength of heart.

This niche acts, therefore, as a valuable strategic and operational means of advancing the tourism sector, attracting invaluable skills, support, exposure and experiences.

Still, there is a need to ensure a healthy approach is taken to voluntourism. The quest to make a difference, even with the best of intentions, can sadly have a negative impact if purpose, projects and people are out of balance.

This is one of the reasons voluntourism has become shunned in some corners. Concerns are valid.

From a project perspective, how is legitimacy of projects managed? How is the well-being of local communities managed with a flow of visitors effectively moving in? How can projects protect themselves from dependency on outside support? How can quality of impact be managed when voluntourists come with varied backgrounds and capabilities? How can travellers signing up for projects know that the project leaders are working in the best interests of the people of the destination, in partnership with the local government and industry?

From a traveller perspective, how sustainable can a contribution really be when travellers are participating in projects for short periods of time? How can completion of projects be planned when traveller flows are inconsistent?

And of immense importance, how can the dignity and motivation of local communities be maintained so that they do not feel they are recipients of charity, handouts, and even worse, pity?

For any nation looking to develop voluntourism as a niche within the greater travel & tourism sector, it is critical that the niche be designed with clear operating principles so as to ensure that all projects and project leaders are honouring both the communities being helped and the travellers helping. Measurement and monitoring of projects, within the greater framework of both national development and tourism sector advancement, are a must.

Ultimately, both travellers and destinations need to be clear of the impact they are seeking to make through voluntourism.

At the heart of successful voluntourism is keeping the fundamentals firmly in place, ensuring that doing the right thing is based on doing things right, starting with:

- **Respect:** Voluntourism projects must contribute to the self-respect and shared respect of the people of the community. Cultural awareness and appreciation of those entering into a project is critical. No individual wants to be treated like a project, a charity, or a tourist attraction.
- **Responsibility:** Voluntourists are utilising their holiday time to partake in a project, voluntarily. Still, the tasks behind the projects require commitment to delivery. For this reason building play-time into a project allows voluntourists to get the rest and relaxation they need, while also making the difference they seek.
- **Relationships:** The power of voluntourism rests in the relationships which are formed between the voluntourists and the people of the projects in which they participate. The work matters, but it is the effect that it has on the people, both through the process of creation and the outcome of the project in its final form, which gives it meaning.
- **Realistic expectations:** The ability to make a real difference must be realistically examined *vis a vis* the time and energy a voluntourist is able to commit to a project. Voluntourists should not expect to change the world in two weeks of teaching a child a language. Voluntourists should seek to be stitches within a greater community development fabric. Important, strong, colourful stitches.
- **Results:** Voluntourism projects need to have clear goals and metrics to ensure delivery is achievable, impact is sustainable. Visible results are critical to yield a valuable harvest. That said, the simple act of planting seeds of hope, confidence, inspiration and appreciation can have an impact far outlasting a period of a few days of project activity.

When structured and managed carefully and comprehensively voluntourism can play an invaluable role in destination development, economically, socially and sustainably. Importantly, voluntourism is a mirror of the desire of people to come closer, making rich, meaningful connections to people and places around the world. Because it's the right thing to do.

CHAPTER 17

CONSERVATION – TOURISM FOR THE LONG TERM

In that time-standing-still moment the almost silent sound of twigs crackling underfoot seemed so loud that it caused a sudden, anxious catching of breath. The tracker looked back with a clear, concerned question in his eyes – "Are you okay?"

"Sorry. I'm fine. Keep going" Pam whispered in response, timid eyes meeting his stare. An hour had passed. All sense of orientation was gone. Yet the tracker knew the terrain of the national park as well as his own, precious backyard. Trust and proximity to the tracker slashing his way through the thick vegetation were all that was required, she thought. And the park and expedition fees. The price of admission, high compared to other national parks, was worth every single cent. Not only did it allow access (limited to control tourist flows) to this breath-taking, very remote corner of the country and continent, it went towards ensuring that the magnificent creatures under its forest canopy remained protected. Their home kept safe for them. Because this is their home. She was merely a very fortunate visitor.

With each slow, steady, thoughtful step gingerly taken through the heavy, sauna-humid forest of the mountains of Rwanda, the intensity of excitement grew. Nettle bushes stinging through layers of clothing created a thrilling sensation – the prick of pain quickly turning into a child-like feeling of awe in actually being where the nettles sting, where the forest dripping with vines and vegetation thrives, where the ground bounces with plush carpet-like mosses. The place where Dian Fossey once walked. And where the Silverback will soon charge to reveal his family of gorillas having been located!

Now, years on, those moments are still so vivid, so real. The sounds, scents, stings and surges of excitement can still be felt. They were truly moments of a lifetime. Along with the immense, rare blessing of being there, in their world, on their terms.

It was a feeling more alive then any other moment in Pam's life. And, importantly, she also knew she was making a direct contribution to their lives, contributing to their survival.

Because they were there first.

Super-natural moments are found all over the world. Their beauty, their power, and their sense of blessing, are caused by a combination of factors critical to the creation of experiences which go beyond adventure – they reach into the space where words such as *'magic'*, *'wonder'*, *'awe'*, *'humility'*, *'authentic'* and *'purity'* live. Where lives change perspective. Where tears fall because you are there.

At the heart of these incredible moments of discovery is remoteness – quiet, still remoteness. The remote chance of not just being there, but of discovery occurring:

- Catching a glimpse of baby gorillas playing like schoolchildren high up in the canopy of trees deep within the Central African mountain forest.
- Spotting the shadow of a whale nearing the boat hovering patiently in the intense blue waters of the reef.
- Hearing the deep, baritone cracking of a glacier in what feels like stretched seconds before a mass of ice crashes into the frigid Arctic waters that the polar bears call 'home'.

And yet, for all of the beauty and wonder, such remarkable places are disappearing. Each and every day as the world undertakes pursuits for a better way, the lives of other precious creatures and ancient creations of our world become threatened.

How can this happen? How can it be possible that some of the world's natural riches are being lost to us, and the next generations of travellers?

Even more importantly, how can leaders in global tourism ensure that conservation is not just a policy, but an enduring philosophy?

To enter into the remotest, richest places of exploration, understanding and discovery means, by its very nature, disturbance of a natural world. Natural environments, natural eco-systems and natural habitats become unnaturally exposed when they become accessible to travellers. The risks are real. Animals may become frightened off. Food supplies killed off. Reef structures broken off. Free-growing space sold off. Waters polluted.

The here and now destroyed.

For all of these reasons, and more, tourism conservation – *actively preserving and protecting the place, people and promise of the destination* – is critical to the long-term health and well-being of the destination as an environment, as an economy.

Conservation is everyone's responsibility. The well-being of the destination is not only the responsibility of the tourism sector – it is also the responsibility of the tourist. And ultimately economic prosperity for the destination through tourism must ensure that growth occurs holistically.

With tourism yielding such distinct and essential economic and social benefits, it is understandable why the sector is generating such excitement. Tourism destinations, both those new onto the global tourism stage and those already well established on same, look to the sector as a solid, highly valuable and deeply meaningful way of developing the economy of the destination.

These benefits can make it tempting for governments to throw open the doors to tourism, reaping as many of the rewards of the sector as soon and as long as possible.

Because of these temptations understanding the concept of *sustainability* becomes critical to tourism.

As much as tourism can bring prosperity, purpose and pride to a destination, so too can it take these benefits away.

With increases in arrivals of leisure and business travellers to a destination, tourism has the potential to cause damage to a destination's value and values system, as a result of:

- over-use of infrastructure without re-investment back into maintenance and renewal critical to the 'engineering' of the destination.
- excessive exposure of natural elements and attractions causing erosion and/or eradication of the environment and ecosystems unique to the destination.
- forfeiting of cultural codes and/or principles for the sake of tourist comfort, tourism-generated money and destination competitiveness, ultimately creating a local tourism culture based on short-term personal gains and greed.

- creation and magnification of seasonal peaks and troughs in tourism industry activity, causing destabilisation in the sector's contribution to the economy and employment.

With these risks in mind, governments and private entities are realising the importance of adopting an approach to tourism growth that ensures long-term destination development grounded in:

- **Responsibility:** Encouraging and stimulating tourism growth in a way which builds the industry for the enduring benefit of the destination as a whole – its product, its people, its proposition and its profile.
- **Accountability:** Absolute respect for, and ownership of, the impact of the sector on the destination at economic and social levels.
- **Legacy:** Maximising tourism sector opportunity today for the long-term benefit of the destination, its stakeholders and its visitors.

What are the core elements of conservation that need to be considered? It begins with the following:

- **Essence:** The core proposition which uniquely, competitively and proudly defines the destination as a brand and experience.
- **Earnings:** Revenues and investment generated directly and indirectly from tourism activity.
- **Economy:** Inter-related, inter-dependent sectors which work together to service and support the tourism industry.
- **Employment:** On-going, year-round job creation of the sector.
- **Environment:** Safety, stability and survival of the natural surroundings of the destination.
- **Eco-systems:** Natural eco-systems which inhabit the destination's land, water and air environments.
- **Equity:** The sense of value and worth of the destination, financially and emotionally.

Conservation is fundamentally important to the long-term viability, credibility, authenticity and productivity of the tourism sector.

Ultimately, conservation is a reflection of a *measurable* approach to sector growth and development which focuses and invests directly into ensuring on-going strengthening of the core elements of the destination, for the next generation of travellers.

And even more so, for the next generation of wildlife.

It is not only about policy and strategy. It is a duty.

ACKNOWLEDGEMENTS

For the first time in the entire process of writing this book, I am at a loss for words. How does one possibly begin to say *"Thank You"*?

Writing this book has been a true labour of love. And at times a mission, involving a number of people to whom I owe immense thanks for their support, their patience, their challenge and their faith.

And so, speaking unedited...

To start, the characters in the stories at the start of each chapter. The names of these characters are the names of people who have made the story of my life, thus far, one of great adventure, love and learning. If people are the punctuation of our life's story, each one of these precious people is an exclamation mark.

To the wonderful group of people who worked to ensure that the finished product was produced, packaged and polished, ready for reveal: Asher Hung, Ramsey Frazier, Holly Rosen, Viv Gordon, Sue Luck, Shaun Viljoen and Larry Katz. My sincere thanks for all of your time, trouble and attention to the tiniest details.

To all of the contributors to this book, especially the UNWTO, WTTC, CNN and TTC, thank you. Behind each of your powerful acronyms I have been so very blessed to find colleagues and friends whom I genuinely admire, respect, and am honoured to work with. Thank you for inspiring my best work.

To David Bridgman, for that fateful day of May 23, 2002 when, in your offices at the World Bank, you asked me a question re. destination R.O.I. – a question which put me on my path and turned my profession into my vocation.

To Lee Thomas. Somehow you knew...

To my family, my thanks.

And to Al Merschen. You are the force that turned a spark into a flame, and a comfortably invisible ghostwriter into a published author. Thank you, for inspiring (and pushing and challenging) me to be my best me. #

CONTRIBUTORS

Sujit Banerjee, former Secretary, Ministry of Tourism, Government of India, and current Secretary-General, WTTC India Initiative

Bruce Bommarito, Senior Vice-President and Chief Operating Officer of the United States Travel Association, USTA

Marc Collins, former Minister of Tourism of Tahiti

Melanie de Souza, General Manager International Marketing, Tourism Victoria, Australia

Diana Ee Tan, former President of Raffles Hotels and Resorts, current Board Member of Singapore Tourism Board, Member, Advisory Council, School of Hospitality, Republic Polytechnic, Singapore and the Academic Board of SHATEC Institutes

Geoffrey JW Kent, Founder and Executive Chairman, Abercrombie & Kent; Chairman, World Travel & Tourism Council

Juan Carlos Ventura Pimentel, Director of Marketing and Strategic Communications, Ministry of Economy of the Federal Government of Mexico

Dr Laurine Platzky, Deputy Director-General, 2010 FIFA World Cup Co-ordinator in the Department of the Premier, Western Cape, South Africa

Rani Raad, Senior Vice-President and Managing Director, CNN International Ad Sales and Business Development

Dr Taleb Rifai, Secretary-General, United Nations World Tourism Organisation UNWTO

Christopher Rodrigues CBE, Chairman, VisitBritain

Brett Tollman, President & CEO, The Travel Corporation

Gavin Tollman, President & CEO Trafalgar Tours

Alan Winde, Minister of Tourism, Finance and Economic Development, Provincial Government of the Western Cape, South Africa

END NOTES

[1] Source: Deutsche Bank Research, EU Monitor, 76 August 2, 2010

[2] Capgemini/Merrill Lynch Financial Advisor Surveys 2007, 2008, 2009, 2010

[3] http://unwto.org/en/about/tourism

[4] http://www.travelwires.com/wp/2010/01/global-travel-trends-for-2010-according-to-rhino-africa/

[5] www.washingtontimes.com/news/.../curl-cost-nyc-weekend

[6] Oxford Economics' *Return on Investment of U.S. Business Travel Study*, 2009

[7] GoGecko, Volunteer Travel Insights, 2009, page 11

INDEX